AF615714

Paul Cézanne

Trewin Copplestone

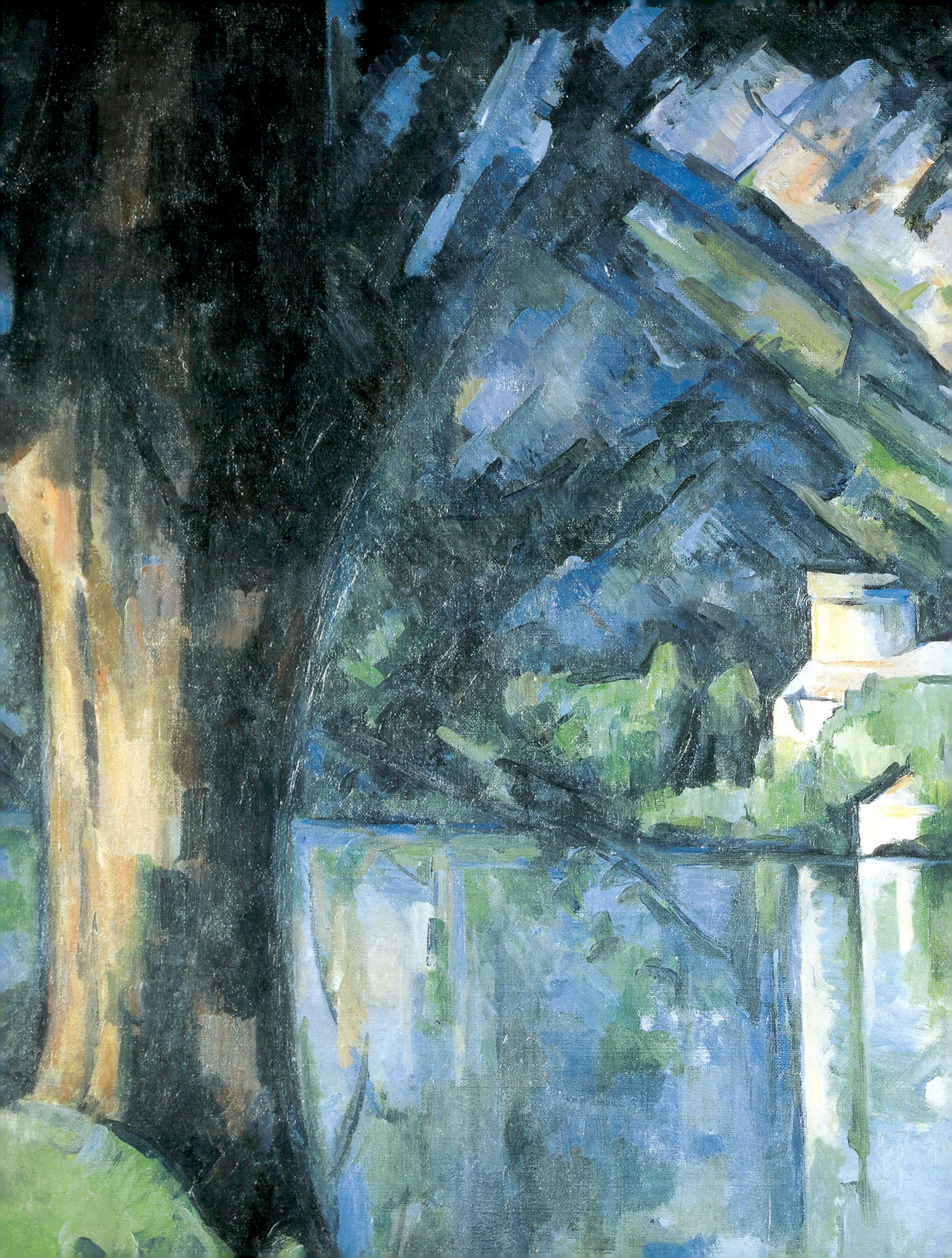

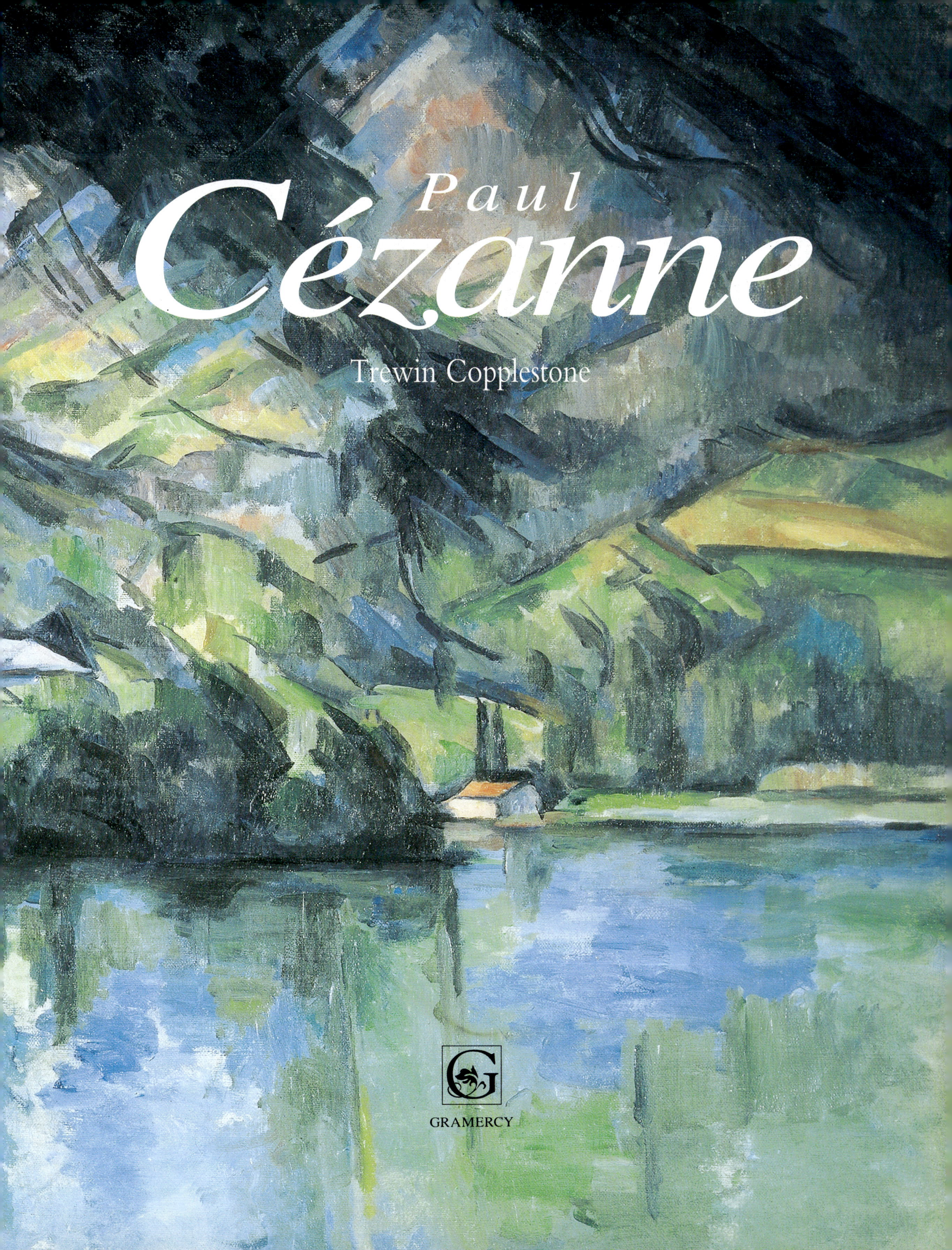
Paul
Cézanne
Trewin Copplestone
G
GRAMERCY

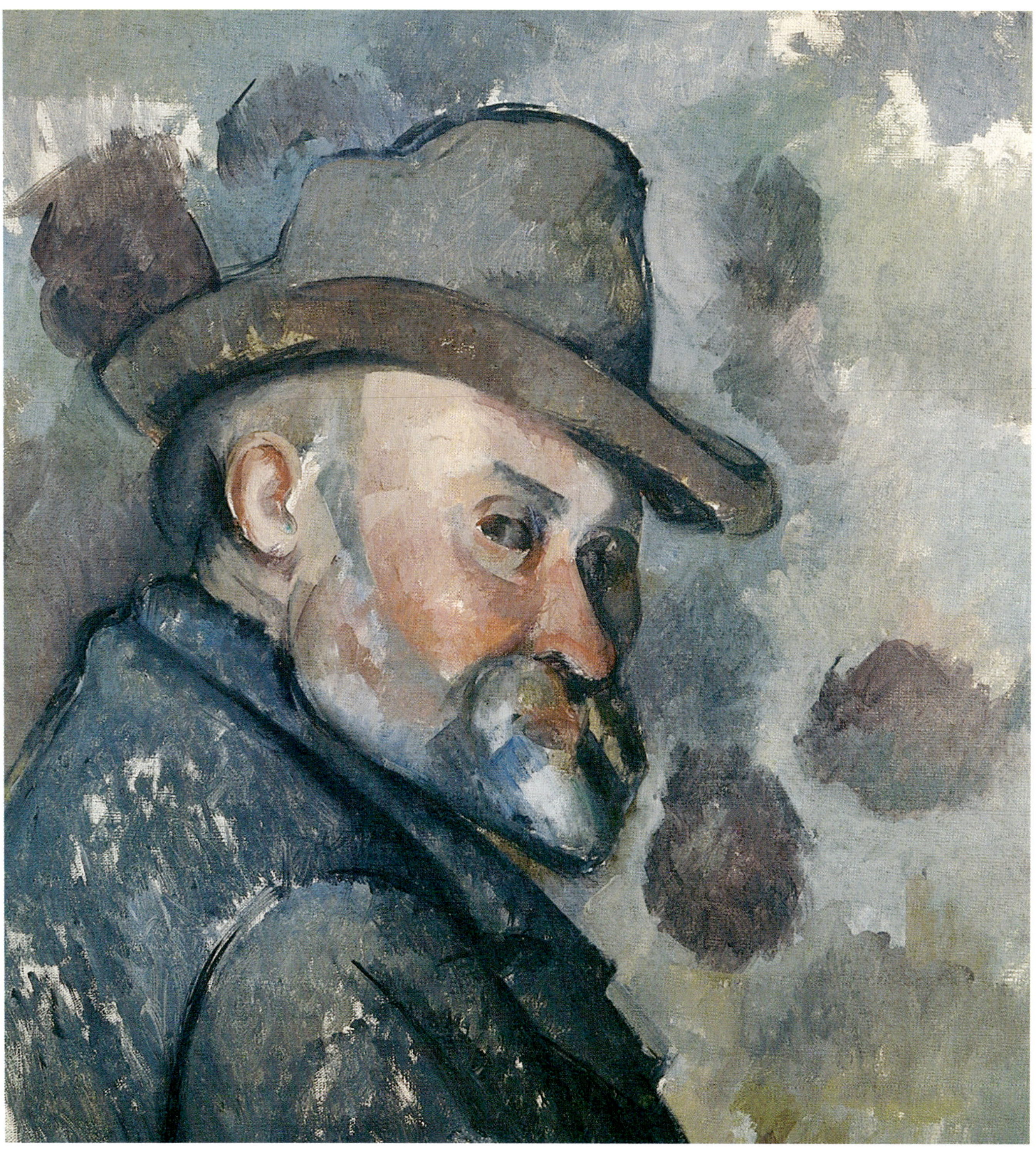

This 1998 edition is published by Gramercy Books, a division of Random House Value Publishing, Inc., 201 East 50th Street, New York, NY 10022
Gramercy Books and colophon are trademarks of Random House Value Publishing, Inc.

Random House New York • Toronto •London • Sydney • Auckland
http: / / www.randomhouse.com/

Printed in Italy

ISBN 0-517-16064-1

10 987654321

LIST OF PLATES

PLATE 1

Paul Cézanne (1839-1906)

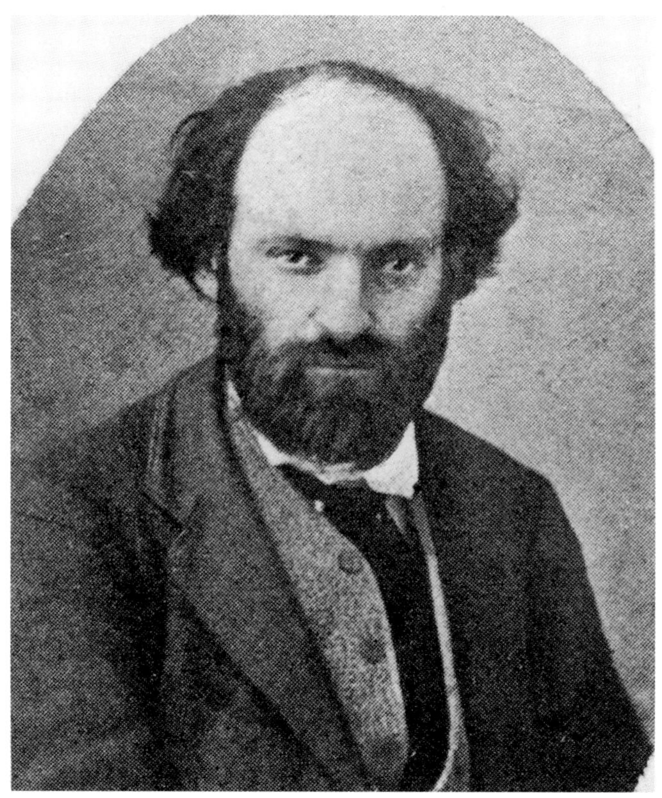

At times, when one reads art critics or historians of 20th-century art, it may seem that the whole structure rests on a foundation called Cézanne. The first movements of the century, Fauvism and Cubism, were led respectively by Matisse and Picasso, and both, despite very different approaches to painting, claimed Paul Cézanne as their mentor and source of inspiration. It is certain that the qualities discerned in Cézanne's work by almost all writers have been seminal to many of the varied directions that painting has taken in the last 100 years, not only in Europe but worldwide as art has become an international enterprise. That Cézanne is the epic icon from which so much of 20th-century art derives its faith and inspiration is somewhat surprising when one examines his decidedly unheroic life in term of positive action or open revolution. Cézanne was never a leader as were many of the French painters – Ingres, Delacroix, Manet or Monet in his own day, Picasso, Matisse or Mondrian in this century. And yet his pre-eminence is hardly disputed and his influence persists.

One may go further and say that Cézanne's reputation is all the more surprising when one recognizes that his art is both difficult and not as immediately attractive to the observer as, for instance, the works of Monet or Degas; neither do they offer the challenge and drama of a Van Gogh or a Gauguin. To add yet one more element of difficulty: he is what is often described as a 'painter's painter'. In other words, it is considered that many, if not most, of his painterly qualities can only be initially appreciated by fellow professionals; for the ordinary picture-lover there often remains the underlying uncertainty of the real value of his work. It is certainly true that he did not have the fluency of drawing or the easily absorbed subject-matter of his contemporaries. Since his death there has been a great deal of eulogistic writing, but there has also been caution and, in a few cases, dismissal. And then one looks at the sale values and asks oneself what there is in these works that explains the prices they command.

Altogether then, a great but difficult painter, whose work, it appears, must be explained before it can be appreciated and enjoyed, and even then one wonders if enjoyment is the right word to identify the experience. It should be said that painting is a language of the eye that appeals to both the visual sense as well as the mind. It is not literature nor is it photography. It has often been said that if a picture could be entirely translated into words, leaving nothing to be communicated, it would not have used its own visual language to make an essential statement.

It is consequently important to attempt to identify what Cézanne's achievement actually was. This is not easy. At a conference concerned with art education at the Institute of Contemporary Art in London some years ago,

PLATE 2

Still-Life with Leg of Mutton and Bread

(1865–67)

Oil on canvas, $10^{2}/_{3}$ x $13^{3}/_{4}$ inches (27 x 35cm)

Cézanne's technique in the early work is well illustrated in this painting. He uses a heavy impasto, applied with both brush and (more often) a palette knife, which almost suggests a modelled form in bas relief. As can be seen in the leg of mutton, he used the knife to follow round the form or (with the lower leg) along it to suggest its structure and feeling. It is clearly the work of someone who is discovering the problems of representational painting. The loaf of bread is an almost amorphous mass and the whole work is constructed in a traditional tonal form. It is because it is so far from the recognizable Cézanne that is so admired and studied and one could be forgiven for not identifying it as such. It gives clear evidence of the struggle that Cézanne endured in the process of developing his art.

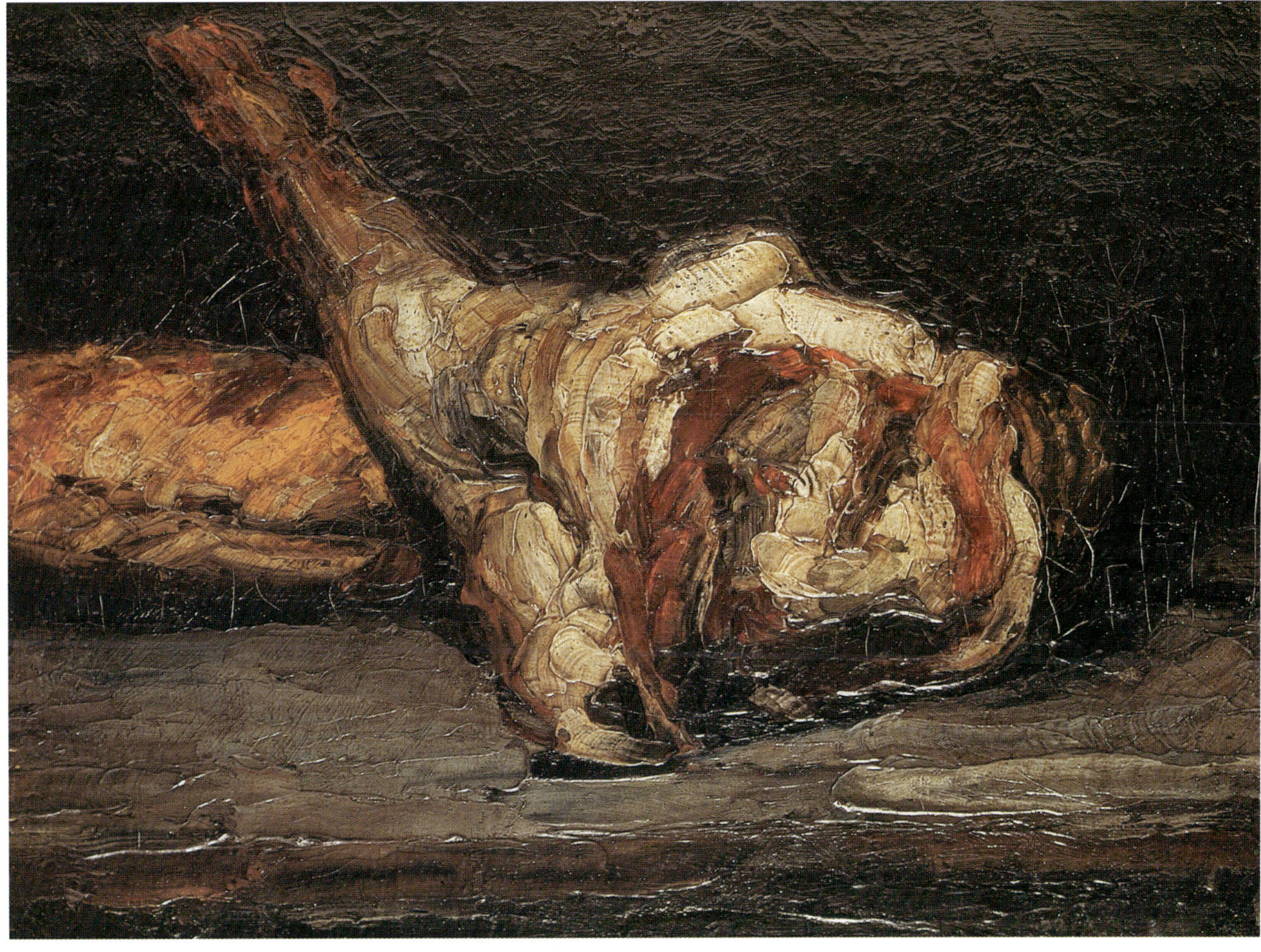

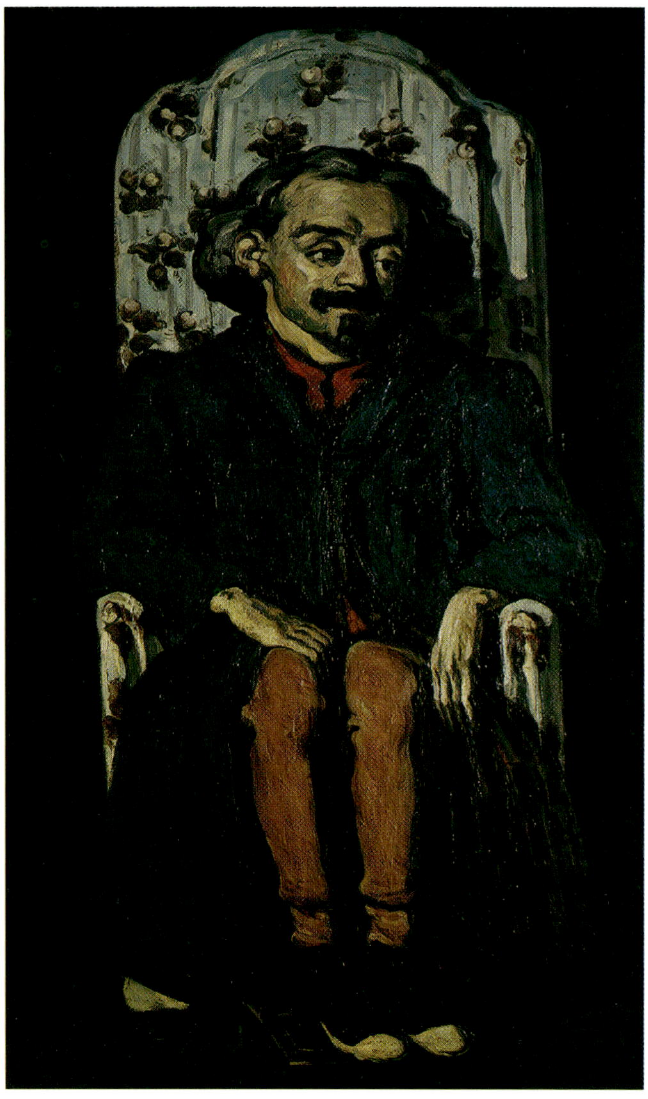

PLATE 3

Achille Emperaire (1869–70)

Oil on canvas, $78^{3}/_{4}$ x 48 inches (200 x 122cm)

Emperaire was a painter friend of Cézanne's and this portrait reveals him as a small, wistful and uncertain figure seated in a pretentious chair. There is no evidence of any animosity between the two, but it hardly seems an affectionate portrayal though the two were good friends for at least ten years. The effect of the composition is curious, the reason being that Emperaire was a dwarf with a large head and a thin body and limbs. Cézanne later described him as 'a burning soul, nerves of steel, an iron pride in a misshapen body, a flame of genius in a crooked hearth'. Cézanne made preparatory drawings for the portrait which shows Emperaire much as Cézanne has described him, one drawing carrying within it almost the vitality of a Bernini sketch.

one speaker complained that it was sad that few art students could explain what the central core of Cézanne's work was, at which the chairman opined that he himself was not sure that he could, and to complete the circle the speaker himself confessed that he was not sure he could either. This may act as a salutary warning. Most students of Cézannes's work agree that it was seminally important and are able to adduce reasons, make perceptive comments, examine the effect of associations, explain his technique, quote his own observations on art and analyse his paintings; but even when aggregated, these elements do not fully explain the reverence and establish the pre-eminence in which he is held. There is a revealing 'for instance'. He is often claimed to have been the principal influence in the origins of Cubism (which he undoubtedly was), but in establishing this, a line written by Cézanne to Émile Bernard in 1904 is often quoted: ' ... treat nature by the cone, sphere and cylinder.' Not, one notes, the cube. But throughout Cézanne's work, the sense of a structural geometry is evident as well as the careful and tentative intellectual underbuilding towards what he called his *motif* – his *petite sensation.* Nonetheless, shorn of all the academic, scholarly dissection and aesthetic hype, the fact remains that Cézanne has been accorded a place in the hierarchy of art above that of almost all his peers.

To understand why this has happened, and before we attempt to evaluate his qualities and achievements, the background to the development of the art of the 19th century may be helpful. Cézanne was born in 1839. His most significant close contemporaries were born respectively, Pissarro in 1831, Manet in 1832, Degas in 1834, Monet in 1840, Renoir in 1841, Gauguin in 1848, Van Gogh in 1853, Seurat in 1859 and, before Cézanne died in 1906, Matisse in 1869 and Picasso in 1881. When Cézanne was born, the important Neo-Classical movement established by Jacques-Louis David and reaching its apogee in the work of Jean-Auguste-Dominique Ingres, who died in 1867, still dominated the French Salon. By the time he was an adult, Romanticism and the important work of Delacroix, who died in 1863, a year highly significant in French art, had begun to inspire young painters, and independent anti-classical groups were beginning to form.

In 1863, when Cézanne was 24 and living in the south of France, the Salon des Refusés – in which Manet exhibited what was thought to be a scandalous and obscene painting, *Le déjeuner sur l'herbe* – signalled the beginning of

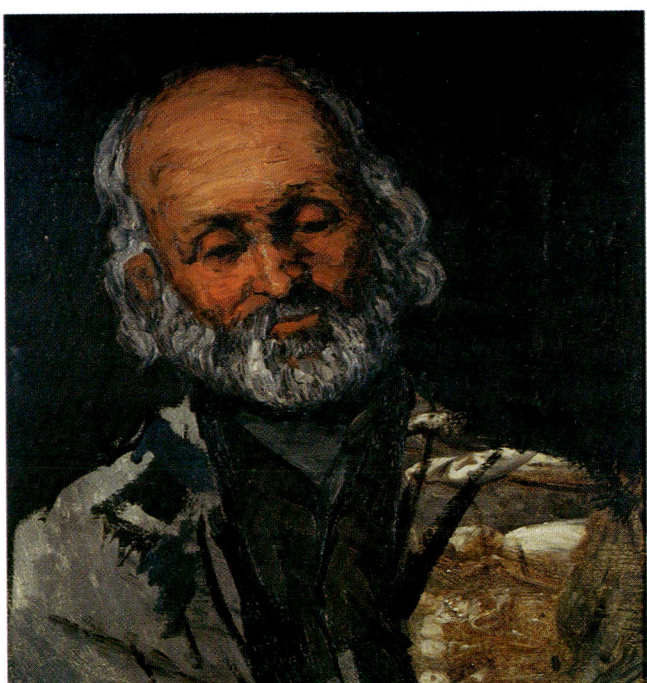

PLATE 4

Head of an Old Man (1865–68)

Oil on canvas, 20 x 18⅞ inches (51 x 48cm)

The characteristics mentioned in the note to plate 2 apply again here, although there are some discernible qualities which will lead to Cézanne's later work; the forehead, for instance, is modelled in a way that shows an interest in expressing the strong dome-like form of the skull. The way the clothes are painted, coarsely and vigorously but incompletely, reveals that Cézanne has painted over another painting, leaving the right lower corner unpainted. (It represents a procession of some kind, as can be discerned by turning the painting on its side.) A painter who at this time sat for a portrait by him, wrote, in a letter to Émile Zola, that 'every time Cézanne paints one of his friends he seems to avenge himself for some hidden injury'.

what was to become the Impressionist Revolution in which Cézanne was marginally and temporarily to participate. It might be noted here that much difficulty and confusion has been caused in trying to include Cézanne as an Impressionist – both to an understanding of Impressionism and to Cézanne himself. It is perhaps wiser to assess Cézanne's real achievement in the period after Impressionism.

In 1870, the Franco-Prussian War between France and Germany began, resulting in the Siege of Paris, changes in the nature of French government, the redesign of the centre of Paris by Baron Haussmann and the dispersion of the art community from the capital – all with considerable cultural damage and disruption. After the war, the Salon reopened and artistic life revived in Paris so that in 1874 the first Impressionist exhibition was held. Reluctantly, and championed only by Pissarro, his friend, Cézanne was admitted but showed only three works. Nevertheless, he was a focus of the most vitriolic criticism for an exhibition which was generally unsuccessful and a critical disaster. Manet, then the leader of those young independents who organized the show, refused to exhibit because Cézanne had been admitted (at that time he had no regard either for Cézanne or his work) and never thereafter showed in the succeeding seven Impressionist exhibitions. Of the three works Cézanne exhibited, *The House of the Hanged Man* (plate 7) is the most significant.

Despite the ridicule, this was the beginning of a series of eight exhibitions (the last in 1886), by which time the Impressionists were recognized and successful; behind their success was the beginning of a development which has become known accurately though not descriptively as Post-Impressionism. This name was surprisingly coined in 1911 by the English painter, critic and writer, and a member of the Bloomsbury group, Roger Fry. Fry himself described it as a 'somewhat negative label' for the exhibition he staged of modern French art at the Grafton Galleries to fill a blank in its programme. It was very successful despite the expectations of its organizers and the fact that Fry was not very familiar with the work he was proposing to exhibit. He visited a number of Paris galleries and dealers, including Ambroise Vollard, Cézanne's dealer, whom he already knew. When it came to naming the exhibition and after discarding a number of suggestions, Fry described it precisely in the phrase: 'Oh let's call them Post-Impressionists; at any event they came after the Impressionists.' The name has stuck and has usually been applied to the generation of younger painters as well as to the later work of some Impressionists. The exhibition, named 'Manet and the Post-Impressionists', opened on 8 November 1910. Manet was Fry's starting-point, although perhaps more appropriately to be described as a Pre- rather than Post-Impressionist, and nine of his works were included. But it was Gauguin (49 works), Van Gogh (25)

PLATE 5

A Modern Olympia (1872–73) below

Oil on canvas, 18 x $21^{2}/_{3}$ inches (46 x 55cm)

A Modern Olympia *represents the exotic element in Cézanne's character which led him into curious historicist exercises. This painting parodies Manet's* Olympia, *the scandalous work exhibited in the 1865 Salon, and it achieved an almost equal* succès de scandale *at the first Impressionist exhibition in 1874. It was one of the three works included and it was because of Cézanne's inclusion that Manet did not exhibit himself. One comment was: 'Cézanne merely gives the impression of being a sort of madman who paints in "delirium tremens".' It was the last outburst of baroque excess as far as the youthful Cézanne was concerned.*

PLATE 6

Still-Life with Green Pot and Pewter Jug (1869–70) opposite

Oil on canvas, $25^{1}/_{3}$ x $31^{7}/_{8}$ inches (64.5 x 81cm)

This painting, together with another from the same time, The Black Clock, *has usually been identified with the change in Cézanne's technique that was leading to the development of his own style and direction. Although during the 1870s he was associated with the Impressionists under Pissarro's influence, unlike them he retained a dominant interest in the still-life as a subject, while they were more interested in landscape or* genre *subjects. For him, the 'grappling directly with objects', undemanding and unchanging, with only the form and relationship to be considered, was a sufficiently inspiring task. While these early works do not perhaps have the grandeur and deeply signifying unity of his mature still-life paintings, they do unmistakably indicate the way his art was moving – away from baroque romanticism to a classical silence.*

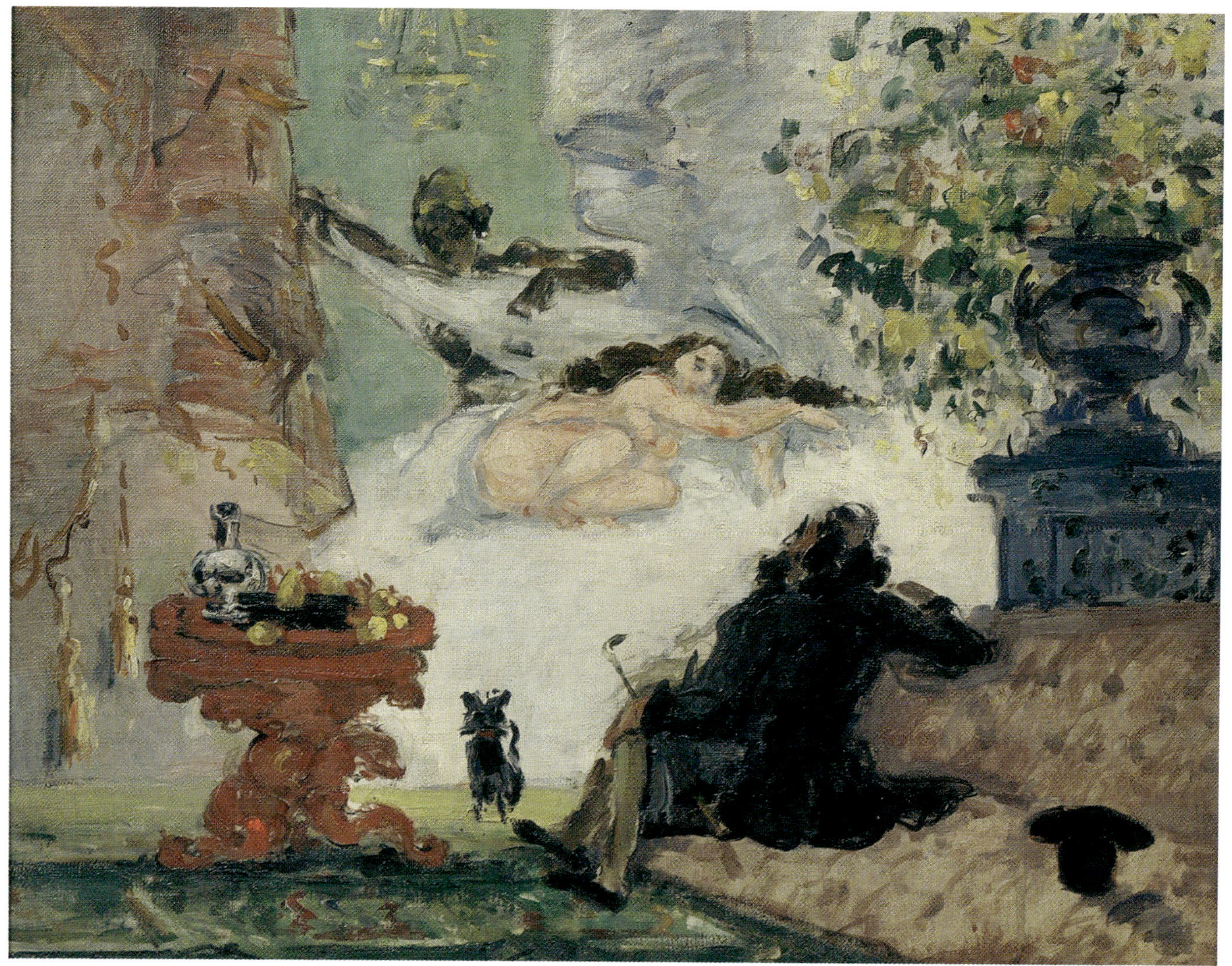

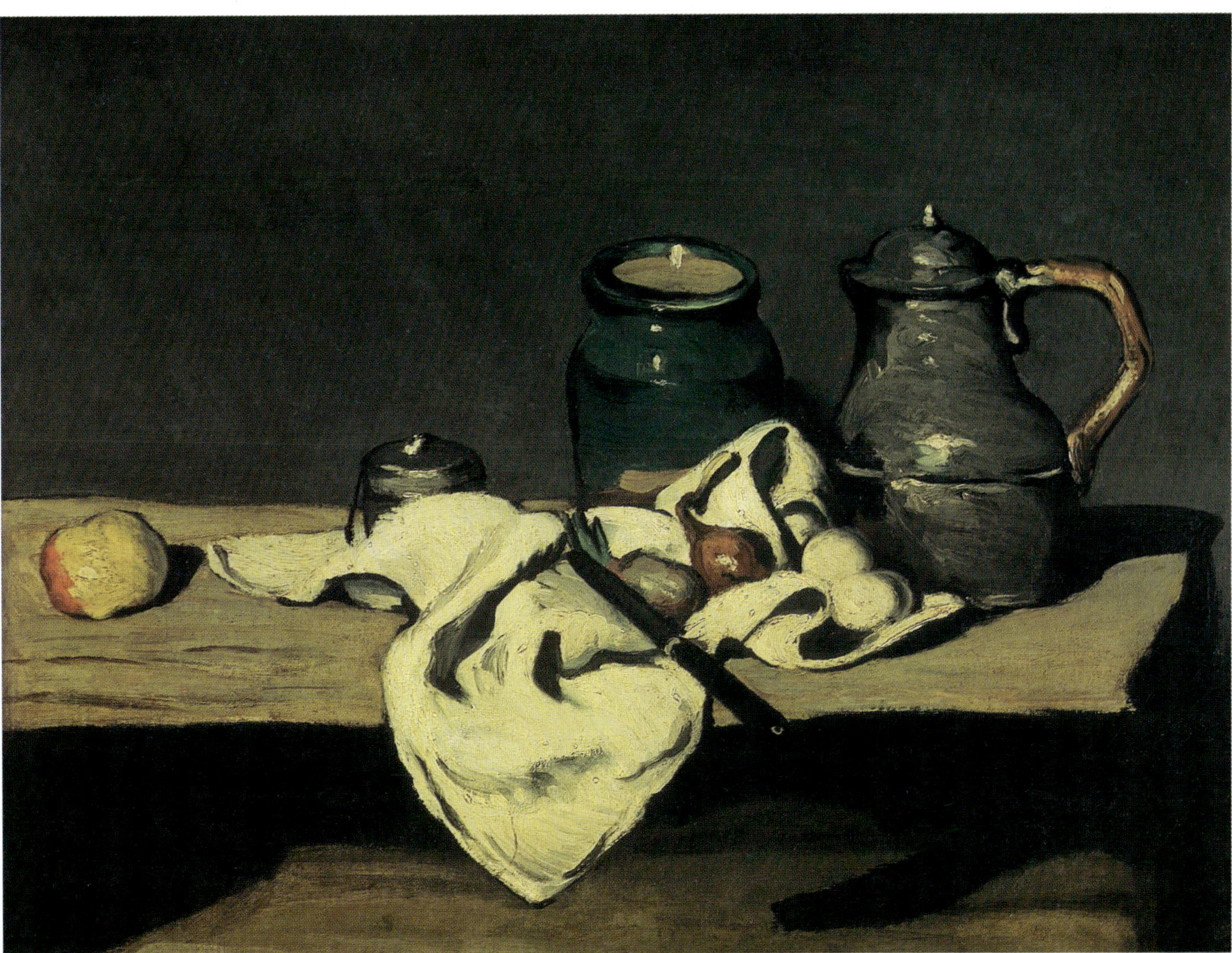

and Cézanne (21) who made up the bulk of the large exhibition. The 20th century was also represented in the works of Fauvists Marquet, Manguin, Vlaminck, Derain and Matisse and Picasso were also included. It is significant that this was the first conjunction of the 19th- and 20th-century forward-looking movements and Cézanne was an important, if posthumous, participant.

There is one perhaps appropriate justification for the title Post-Impressionist as applied to the reaction to Impressionism occurring in the 1880s in that the character of the work of even the acknowledged Impressionists was from that time beginning to change – or already had done so. There were two particular ways in which this might be described: one 'scientifically analytical', the other 'emotionally significant'. Of the four most important (the other three being Seurat, Van Gogh and Gauguin), it is Cézanne who most clearly establishes the potential future programme for the remainder of the 19th and into the 20th century and that gives him his acknowledged pre-eminence. As we have noted earlier, his background and character seemed an unlikely presage of things to come.

Paul Cézanne was born on 19 January 1839 in Aix-en-Provence. His father, Louis-Auguste, was a local hatter who with some enterprise, acumen and good luck had established a successful business in the felt-manufacturing town of Aix-en-Provence just before the boom in felt hats for men and women occurred. He was shrewd and business-like and with two partners had a shop in the main street of Aix. He made a considerable fortune, eventually becoming one of the richest men in town. With this, his ambition increased and, realizing that he could profit more from lending money than selling hats, took the opportunity of buying the local bank when it failed and, under his control, this in turn flourished. Despite his success he was not socially accepted in the town because he had committed the cardinal sin of taking a mistress in the 1830s. Anne-Élisabeth-Honorine Aubert, 16 years Louis-Auguste's junior, became Paul's mother and two years later another child, Marie, was born. A further two years elapsed before Louis-Auguste married Anne and ten years later they had their third and last child, Rose. The Cézannes, even after they had established a regular

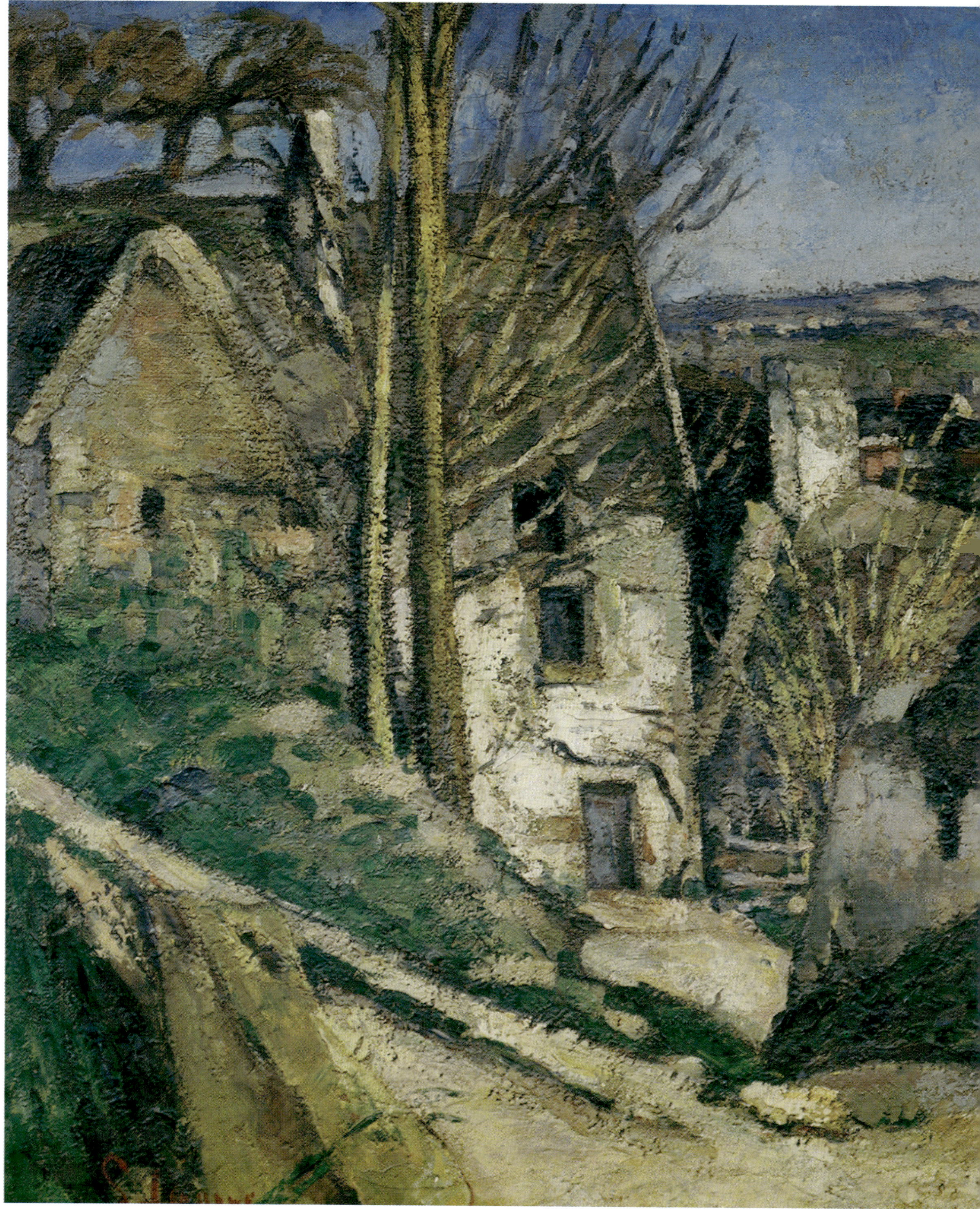

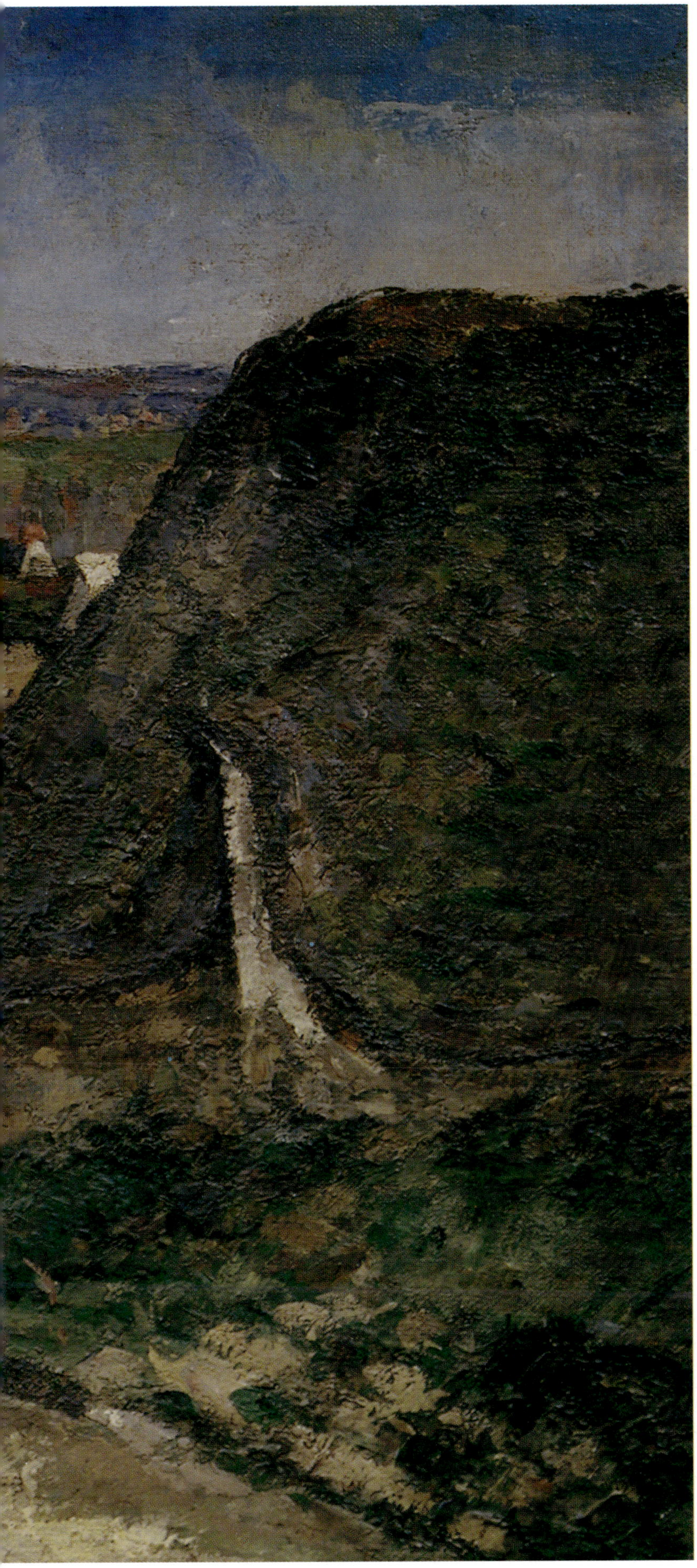

PLATE 7

The House of the Hanged Man, Auvers
(1873)

Oil on canvas, $21^{7}/_{8}$ x $26^{1}/_{4}$ inches (55.5 x 66.5cm)

This painting was also exhibited in the first Impressionist exhibition and a comparison with A Modern Olympia *(plate 5) shows how far Cézanne had come under the influence of Pissarro with whom he had worked in Pontoise in the previous year. This is a considered and objective study, so remarkably different as to seem out of character in such a stubborn person as Cézanne – in fact, Zola once claimed that, 'to convince Cézanne of anything is like teaching the towers of Nôtre-Dame to dance'. The picture, which depicts an attractive house, is of more solid construction than a characteristic 'Impressionist' work might be and, included with them, is already an indication of Cézanne's more pictorially structured work. Although called the house of the hanged man, there is no record of any association with such a person. At that time, Cézanne spent most of the year in Auvers and made daily visits to Pissarro in Pontoise.*

conjugal relationship, remained social outsiders. Louis-Auguste became a recluse though he was loved and admired by his children despite being rejected by the town. Unable and unwilling to reveal or express his emotions, he passed his own lack of self-confidence on to his children, a characteristic which Paul retained throughout his life and which led to many of his actions being misinterpreted.

After a primary education in Aix, Paul became a boarder at the Collège Bourbon where he at first suffered greatly from bullying which, since he was large and strong he overcame, though not without further damage to his self-esteem. At college he made a friend who had a considerable affect upon his life both then and later. Émile Zola, whose father had been an engineer in Aix and had died when Émile was seven, was left almost destitute when his mother failed to recover the substantial monies owed to her husband for engineering work already completed. Émile was sent as a part boarder to the college and, unlike Paul, was small, sharp and outspoken and had not been born in Aix – all crimes according to the young school bullies. Cézanne championed him and the tormenters eventually left Zola alone, so beginning a lifetime relationship which was subject to many vicissitudes and, eventually, a break-up. In 1858, Zola left for Paris and Paul entered the drawing academy in Aix. In the following year, Louis-Auguste bought the country house near Aix

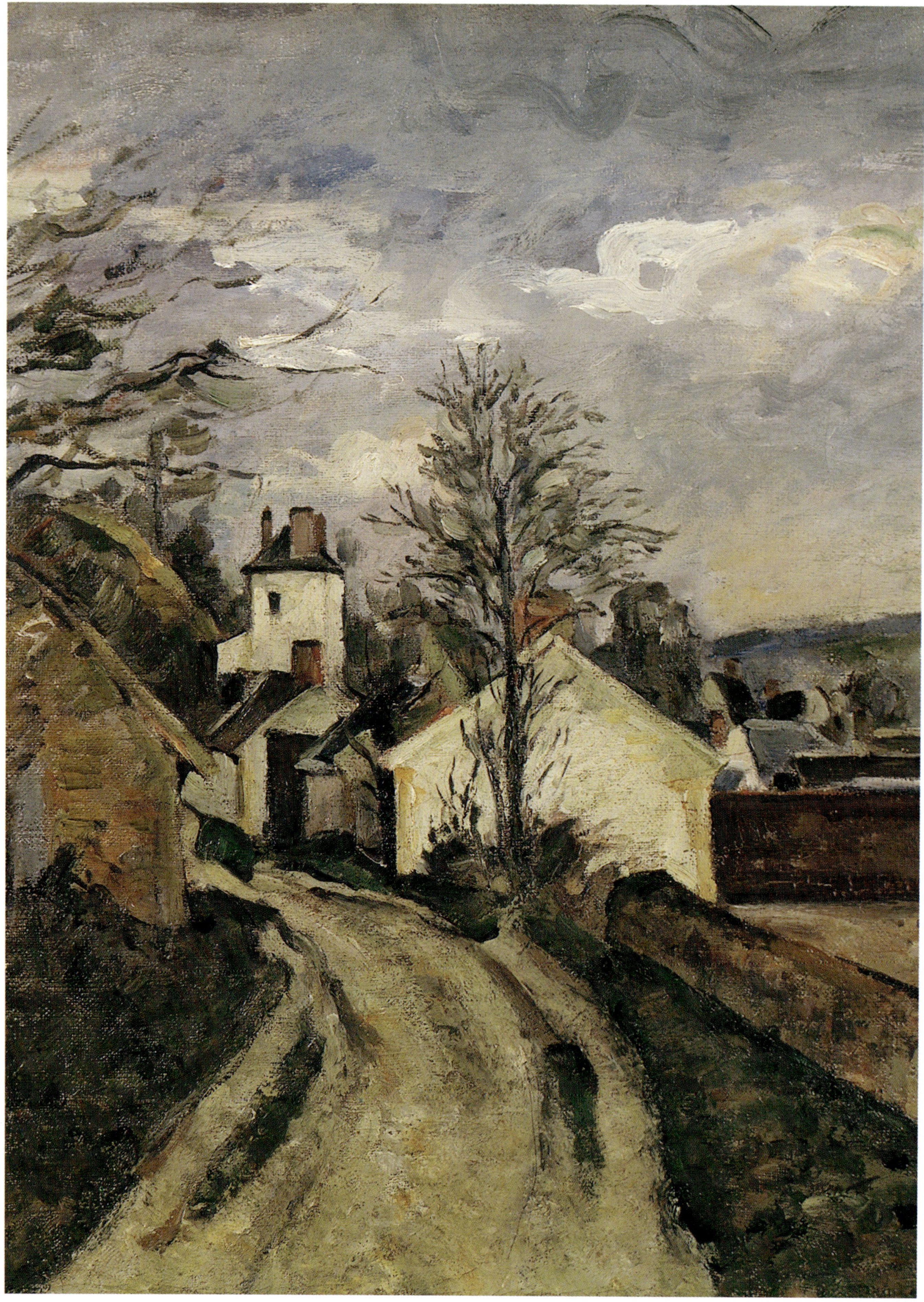

PLATE 8

Dr. Gachet's House in Auvers (c. 1873)

Oil on canvas, 18 x $14^{3}/_{4}$ inches (46 x 37.5cm)

In April 1872, Dr. Gachet bought a property in the rue Rémy in Auvers and Cézanne spent the whole of 1873 in the town with Hortense and their son Jean, making daily trips on foot to Pontoise where he worked with Pissarro who, it will be recalled, Cézanne regarded as his teacher. It was during this period that Cézanne, under Pissarro's influence, came closest to being an Impressionist but (as can be seen here) the structure and geometry of the picture is already significant to him.

PLATE 9

Flowers in a Delft Vase (c. 1873–75)

Oil on canvas, 16 x $10^{2}/_{3}$ inches (41 x 27cm)

PLATE 10

Dahlias (c.1873–75)

Oil on canvas, $28^{3}/_{4}$ x $21^{1}/_{4}$ inches (73 x 54cm)

Painted in Auvers at Dr. Gachet's house, this was retained by the Gachet family until it was donated by them, together with Flowers in a Delft Vase *(below left), and entered the Louvre collection of Impressionism in 1951. Dr. Gachet was an amateur painter himself, exhibiting under the pseudonym of Van Ryssel, and was a friend of Cézanne and other painters, including Van Gogh, who committed suicide while in his care. The dense impasto of this painting, different from the earlier palette-knife applications, is the result of the influence of the remarkable painter Monticelli who became Cézanne's friend, introduced to him by Pissarro. There is a richly manipulated colour quality, given its key by the vibrant white flowers.*

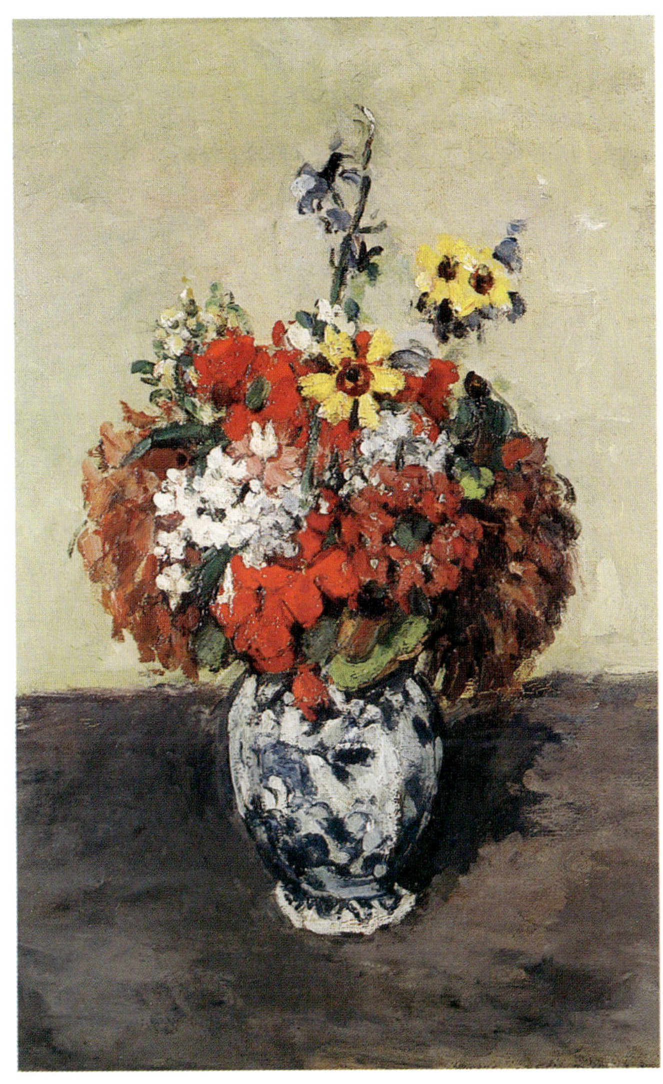

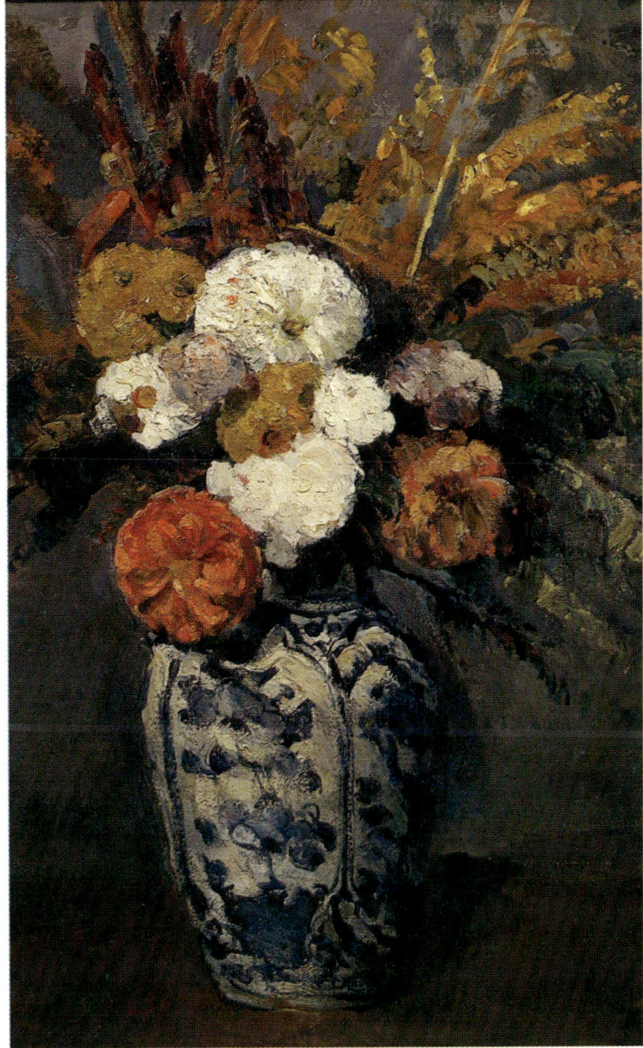

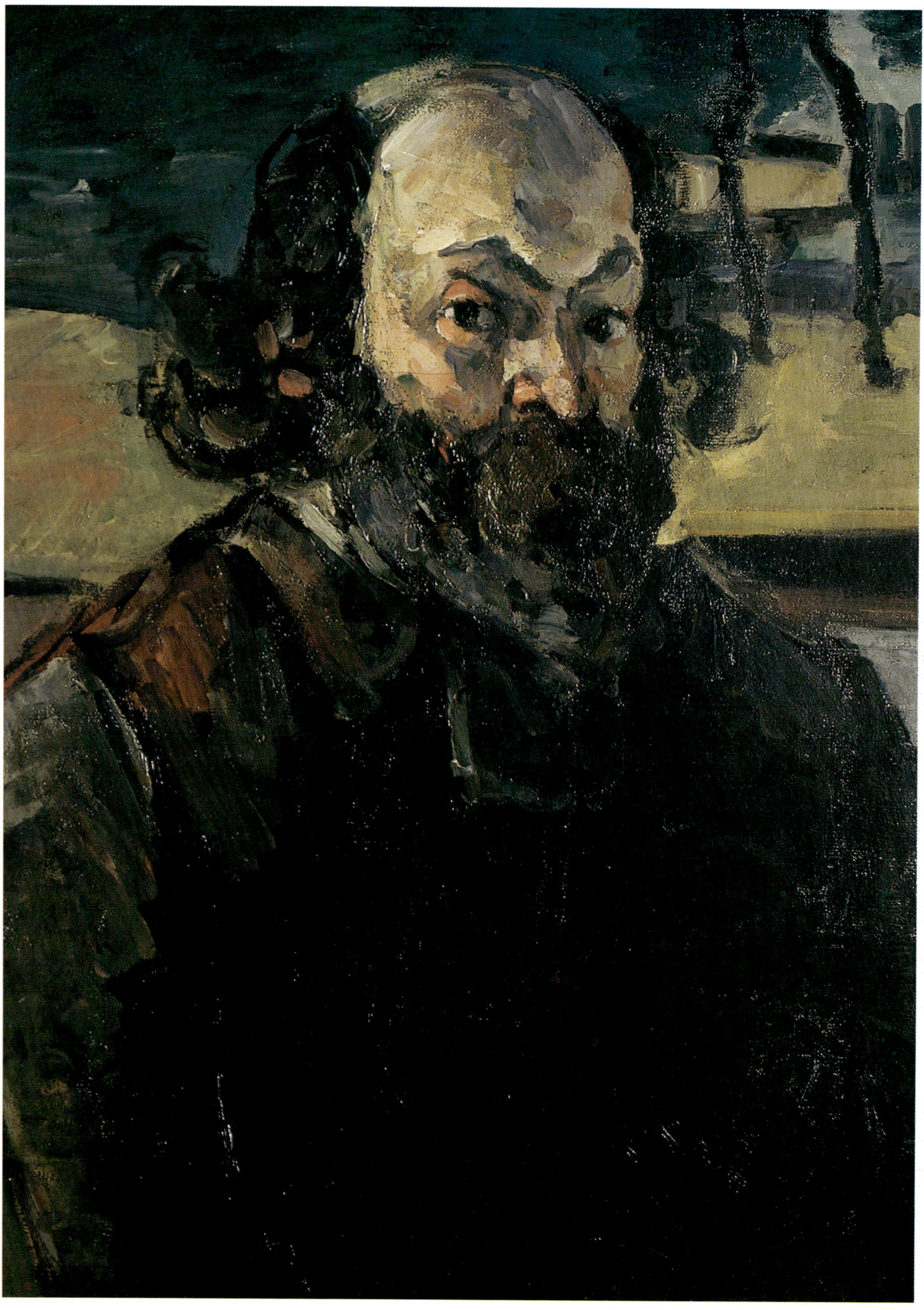

PLATE 11

Self-Portrait (c. 1875)

Oil on canvas, $25^{1}/_{4}$ x $20^{1}/_{2}$ inches (64 x 52cm)

It was only during the 1870s that Cézanne made a number of self-portraits, although there are some drawings and one painting from 1861–62. This one is probably the first of these, although it is difficult to establish a precise chronology. It is an interesting mixture of Cézanne's early and developing approach to paint application. A number of the brushstrokes are forceful and strongly, if vaguely, a directional harking back, while the structure of the dome of the head is painted with searching care; it was a constant preoccupation in his portraits. The painting behind the head is part of an urban scene by Guillaumin, another close friend.

known as Jas de Bouffan around which Cézanne centred much of his early work. Also in 1859, on the instructions of his father, he unhappily and unwillingly began to study law at the University of Aix. But he was now already determined to become a painter and in 1861 he abandoned his law studies and made his first visit to Paris where he met Pissarro, already a professional painter and part of the independent group, at the Atelier Suisse, one of the well known Parisian studios in which professional painters taught the process of painting in the academic tradition. After the first meeting, Pissarro described Cézanne as a 'curious Provençal' – an early example of the effect Cézanne had on anyone meeting him for the first time. Despite first impressions, Pissarro remained a friend and early mentor to Cézanne.

After this visit, Cézanne, under parental pressure, returned to work in his father's bank; but his ambition to become a painter dominated his thoughts and feelings. He took up painting and returned to Paris where he failed entrance to the École des Beaux Arts, was rejected for the Salon every year from 1864 to 1869, and worked in the Atelier Suisse. This unpropitious beginning in a city which was the centre of European artistic life was discouraging, and his relative naïvety and retiring manner did little to further his progress. Nevertheless he persisted, and remained based in Paris until the outbreak of the Franco-Prussian War in 1870, making occasional visits to Aix. As has been noted, he exhibited in the Salon des Refusés in 1863 and was a peripheral figure in the group that met at the Café Guerbois and of which Manet was the leader. He had been introduced by Pissarro who was at that time almost his only strong supporter.

At the outbreak of the war, and to escape from army service, Cézanne went to L'Estaque in 1870, living there with a model, Hortense Fiquet, where their son Paul was born in January 1872. In this year Cézanne went to work with Pissarro in Pontoise, coming under his influence and changing his early heavy pigmental style to a near Impressionist technique. Although this influence was short-lived, it gave Cézanne contact with the Impressionists although only Pissarro regarded him highly. He was beginning to achieve some small reputation as a serious painter, though thought by his peers to be technically unaccomplished, but failed to sell his work and lived off a small allowance from his unconvinced father.

The first Impressionist exhibition opened in the former studio of the famous photographer Nadar on 15 April 1874. Organized by Degas and Monet, it included three paintings by Cézanne of which one, *The House of the Hanged Man* (plate 7), was bought by Comte Doria. After the close of the exhibition a month later, Cézanne spent short periods in Aix and Paris, returning to Aix and thence to L'Estaque. He declined to exhibit in the second Impressionist show (1876) but in the third held

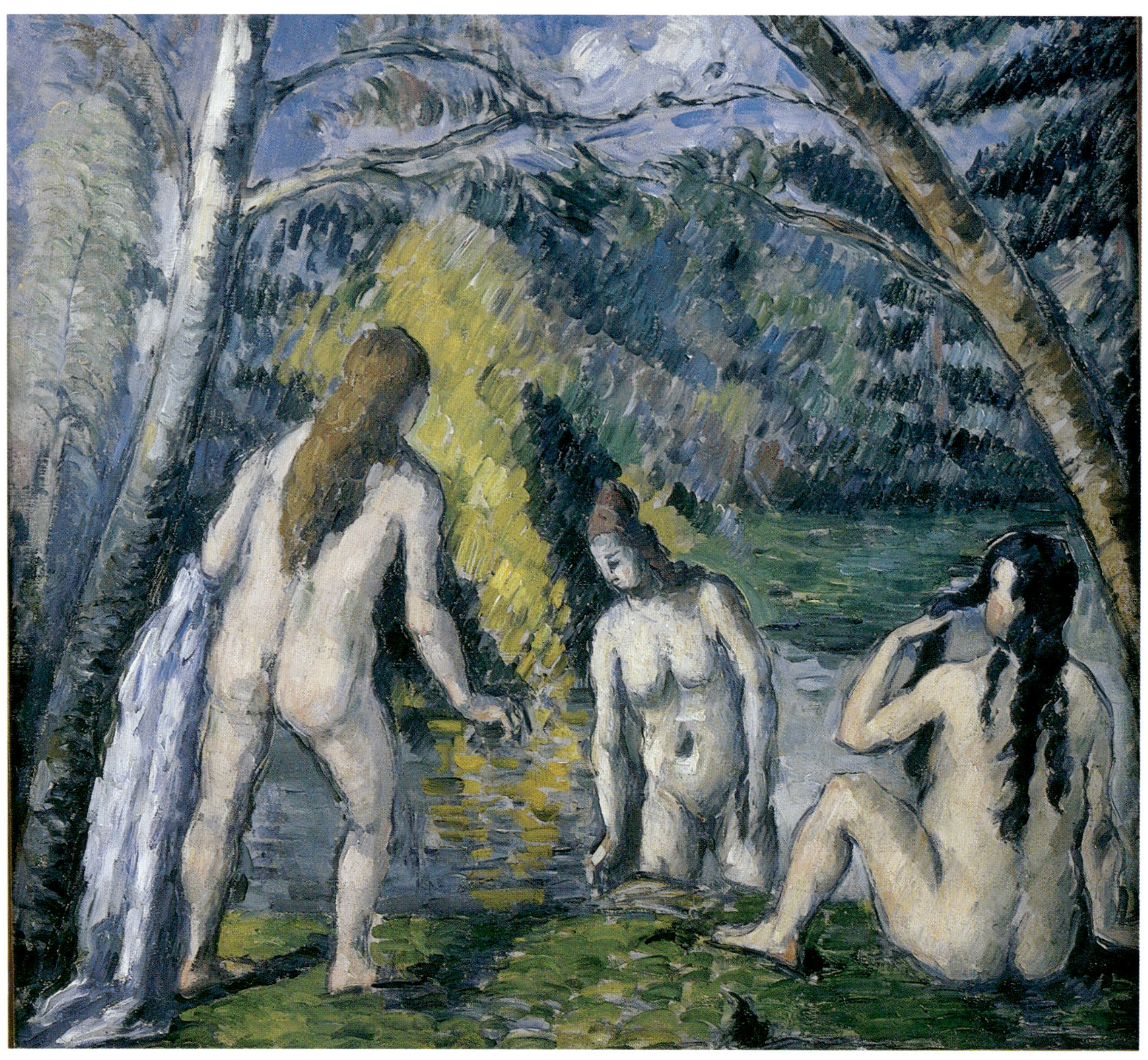

PLATE 12

Three Bathers (1879–82)

Oil on canvas, $20^{1}/_{2}$ x $21^{2}/_{3}$ inches (52 x 55cm)

Matisse bought this painting from Vollard in 1899 and it was donated by him to the Petit Palais in 1936. It has acquired a critical importance in the study of the influence of Cézanne on 20th-century painting. As already noted in the introduction, Matisse was a great admirer and at the time of donating the work wrote to the curator: 'Permit me [to say] *that this picture is of the first importance in Cézanne's oeuvre, for it is the very dense and very complete realization much studied by him in several canvases which, although in important collections, are only the studies that led up to this work.' These series paintings which continued to the end of his life are a significant aspect of Cézanne's method.* (See also plates 45 and 46.)

PLATE 13

Self-Portrait (c. 1880)

Oil on canvas, $17^{3}/_{4}$ x $14^{1}/_{2}$ inches (45 x 37cm)

As already noted, Cézanne painted a number of self-portraits and this example from his maturity reveals how he had developed his structural control and unity to the extent that this is one of his finest portraits. The pictorial relationship between the smooth dome of the solid skull and its opposite in the solid rough beard, and the hinge of the ear that links them indissolubly, creates an image of absolute immutability which makes the painting a separate identity from its inspiration. It is a wonderful extension of the nature of representation which Cézanne took forward from Impressionism and, in turn, from the influence of the Renaissance.

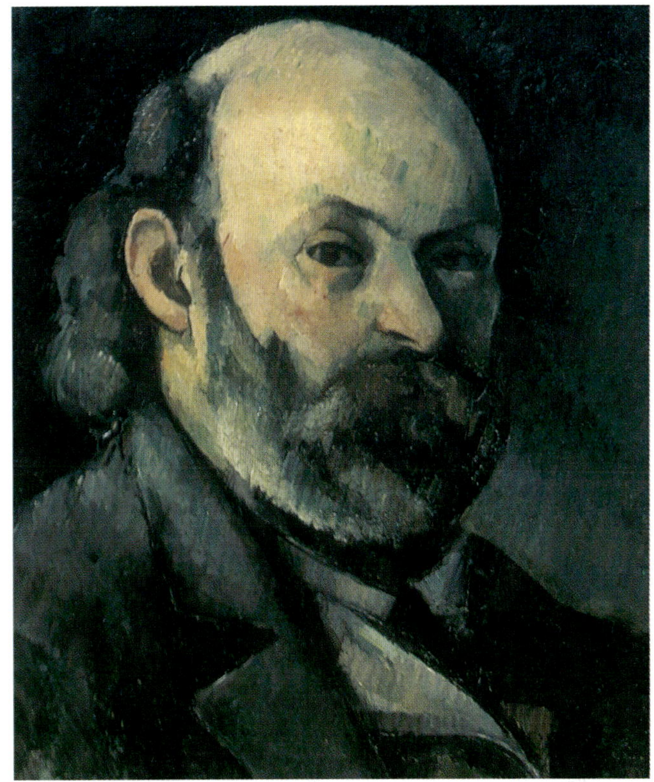

in the following year showed 16 paintings.

Although Cézanne's private life was undramatic and he was not in great financial need, his father had discovered his liaison with Hortense and unsuccessfully tried to break it up. Cézanne's father, despite his financial acumen, retained an essentially peasant attitude towards the arts, could not comprehend his son's intellectual needs, and was disgusted that a man of 40 was not able to support himself. On learning of his son's unconventional domestic situation and despite the fact that he had himself behaved in an exactly similar manner, his father cut his allowance from the modest 200 francs a month to 100, leaving Cézanne impossibly little on which to support his family. He appealed to his friend Zola to find him a job who helped him out financially instead; Zola offered, as he said, to help 'as long as is necessary'. Cézanne asked that the money be sent directly to Hortense who was living in Marseille with their son Paul who was ill.

Through Renoir, in 1875, Cézanne met Victor Chocquet, a customs official, an amateur painter and a collector of Impressionist paintings despite having little money – evidence that these paintings could be bought for no great sum of money. Cézanne painted both Chocquet's portrait and that of his wife. Although still ridiculed by the critics, his painter friends – encouraged by Pissarro – were beginning to realize that this strange and diffident character was not following the same Impressionist course as expressed by Monet, Renoir and Pissarro, but was moving in a personal direction of his own. By the end of the 1870s, Cézanne was spending more time in Aix and less in Paris. He was also working with Pissarro in Pontoise, where he met Gauguin, and in L'Estaque with Renoir. In 1883 he worked for most of the year around Aix and later the same year, in December, was joined in the south by Monet and Renoir. By 1885, he was in Aix or L'Estaque for most of the year to begin a more settled and undramatic period of painting.

The year 1886 was an important one for Cézanne. The last Impressionist exhibition took place in which Cézanne exhibited paintings. For Cézanne, it was the end of an annual event which had become too closely identified with what by then was a popular movement and with which many lesser artists had become associated; it no longer had any relevance to Cézanne or his work which, even from the first, had not truly represented his views. From this time, Cézanne came to be recognized for what he had always been – an individualist in search of his own language.

Three developments in Cézanne's personal life were also of great significance in the same year. Firstly, Zola published his novel *L'Oeuvre*, which caused a rift in his relationship with Cézanne who was deeply hurt by obvious, if not explicit, uncomplimentary references to himself in the central character, Claude Lantier, a painter.

PLATE 14

Female Nude on Sofa (c.1880–82)

Oil on canvas, $16^{1}/_{2}$ x 24 inches (42 x 61cm)

This curious work is part of a study for Cézanne's painting of Leda and the Swan *and includes at a different scale two pears in the top left-hand corner. In the eventual painting, Leda is in the same pose and the Swan replaces the pears. This is Cézanne's version of a voluptuous nude, structured as a landscape or still-life might have been. The result is a somewhat incongruous figure, the doubtless sagging flesh bound into a strict architecture. In the final work, the swan is biting Leda's raised hand. Cézanne was making other nudes studies at this time – usually of male bathers.*

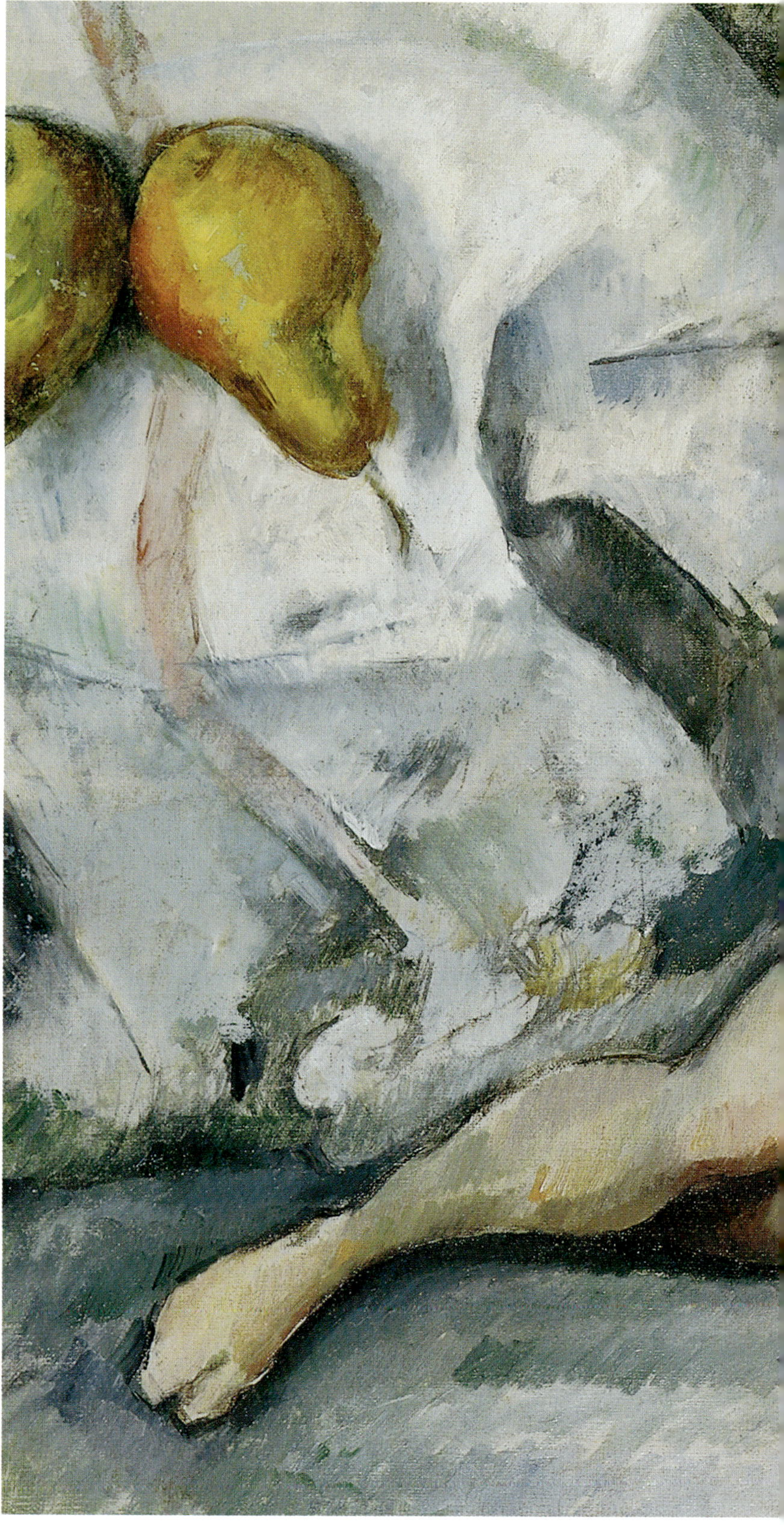

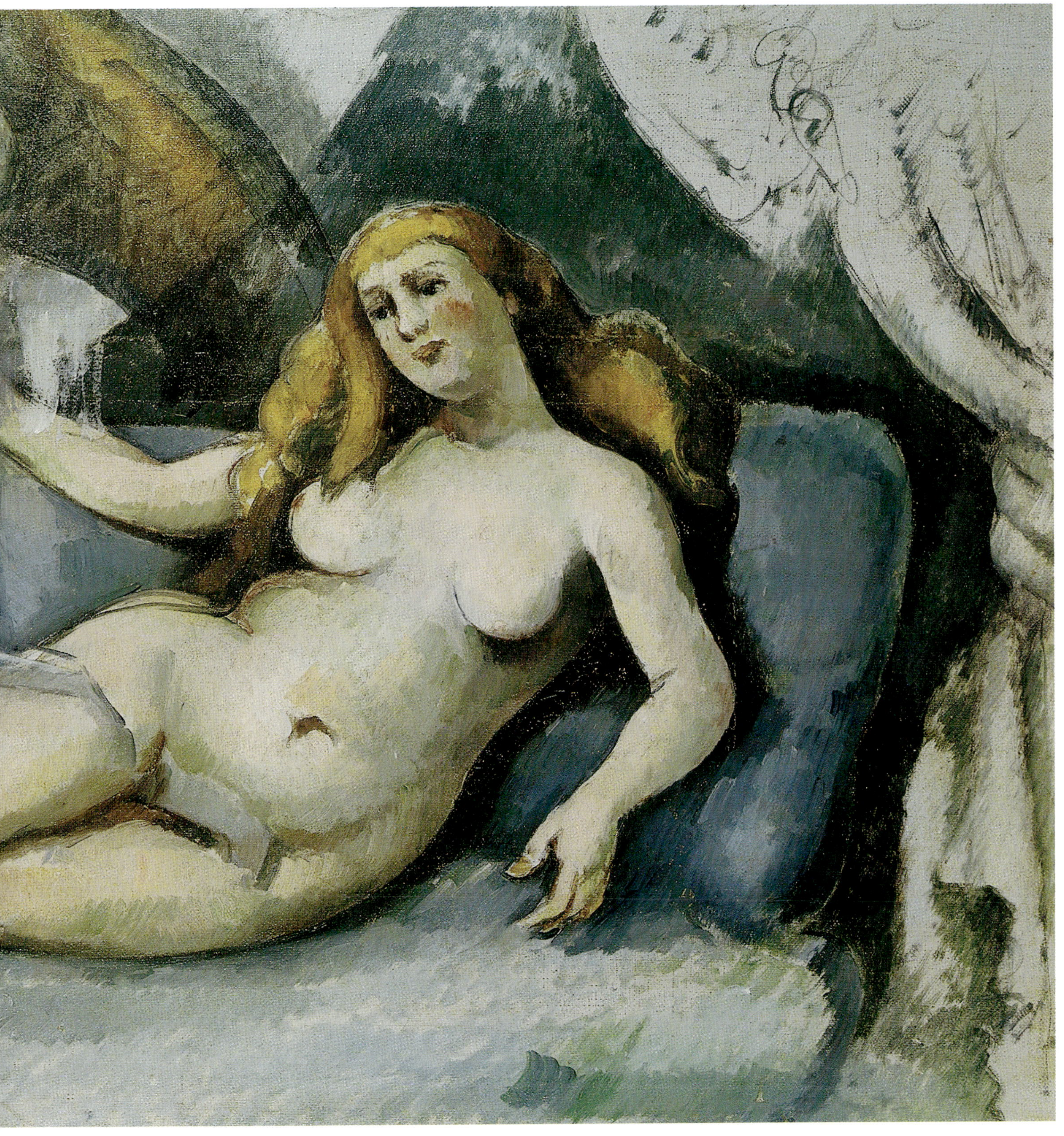

PLATE 15

The Château at Médan (c. 1880) detail

Oil on canvas, $23^{1}/_{4}$ x $28^{1}/_{3}$ inches (59 x 72cm)

Émile Zola, as the result of the success of his novel, L'Assommoir, *was able to buy a house at Médan, near Paris. Naturally Cézanne, his friend, was invited to visit on frequent occasions and during one visit he painted a château from a small island in the Seine that Zola owned. (Zola's house is to the right of the château and not visible in the painting.) As in the two still-life paintings illustrated in plates 16 and 17, this work is in three tonal bands, ranging from the deepest upwards to the lightest. Within the central band there is another which contains the outbuildings of the château with the main building on the right and the vertical trees interrupting the flow of the straggling buildings and providing a tight, interlocked composition. The trees piercing the sky enliven the control and is a frequent solution for Cézanne.*

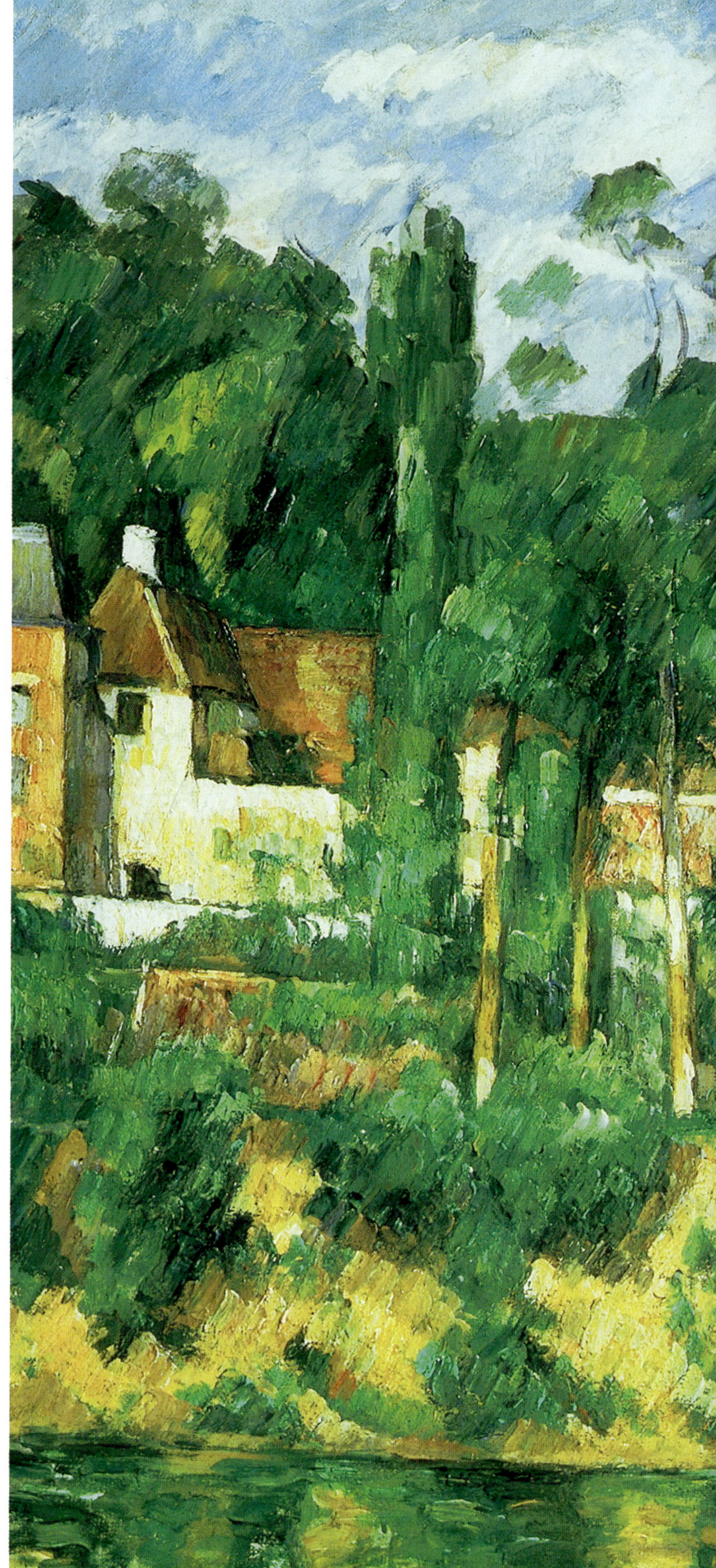

Secondly, he married Hortense in the presence of both his parents which restored their damaged relationship. Thirdly, and later in the same year, his father died, leaving Cézanne an appreciable fortune.

Cézanne's reputation was beginning to grow despite his reclusive life in the south of France and in 1889 Chocquet arranged to have the painting, *La Maison du Pendu* (*The House of the Hanged Man*) shown at the Paris World Fair. In the same year he exhibited in Belgium. His new financial independence enabled him to settle Hortense and their son in Aix, leaving him to pursue his painting wherever he wished. Although well known, his isolation from the centre of artistic life (which was of his own choosing) was turning him into something of a remote and legendary figure. In 1894 he spent the summer at Giverny on the Seine near Paris, the famous home of Monet and the haunt of artists and notable figures in French arts, culture and society. There he met Clemenceau, the great political figure known as the 'Tiger of France', Auguste Rodin, Mary Cassatt (the American Impressionist friend of Degas) and Gustave Geffroy, the critic and writer.

A young American painter, Matilda Lewis, who was staying at the same hotel as Cassatt and Cézanne in Giverny, provides us with a graphic description and character analysis of Cézanne at that time. Quoting Daudet's description of the man from the Midi as 'a man

Continued on page 32

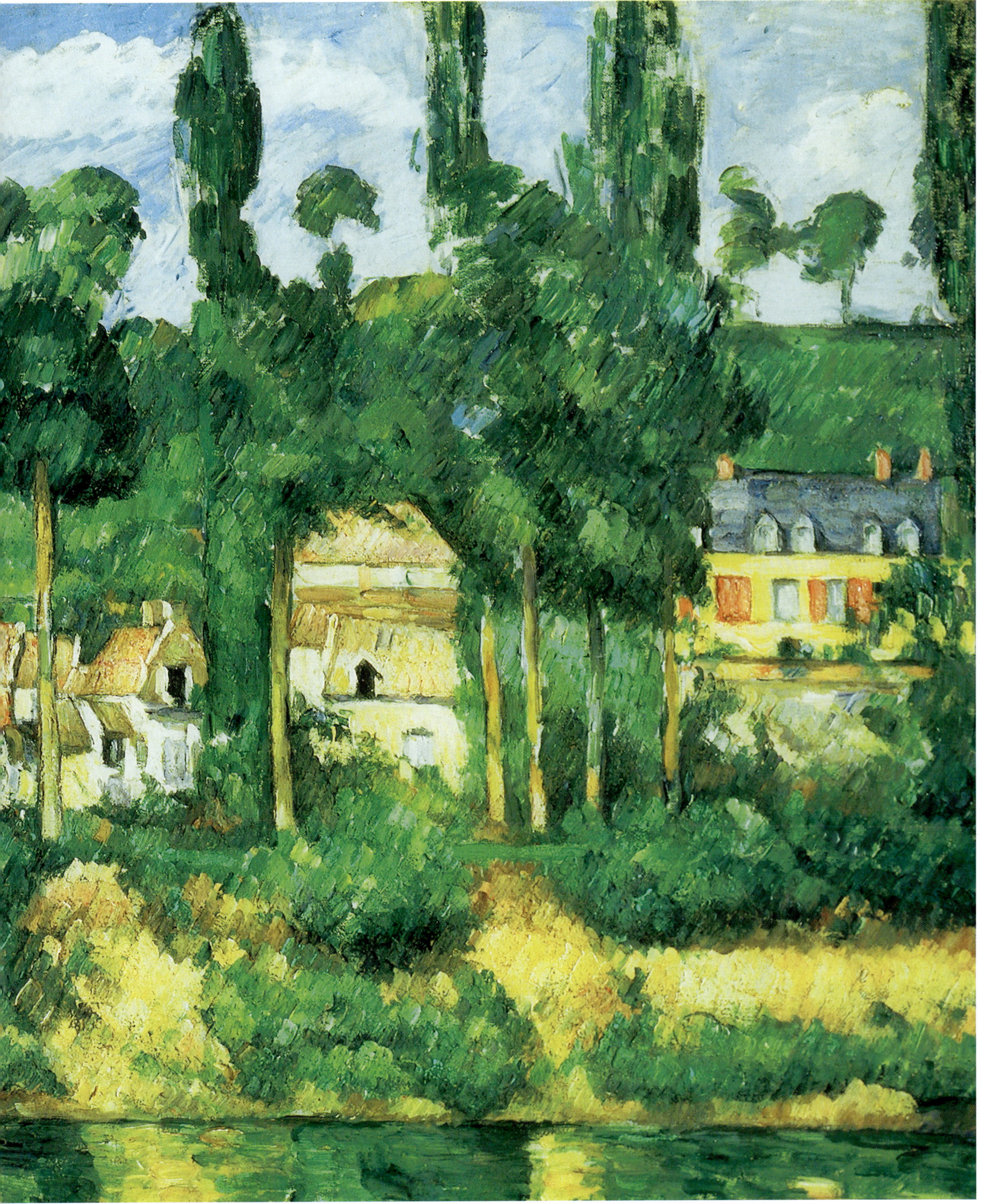

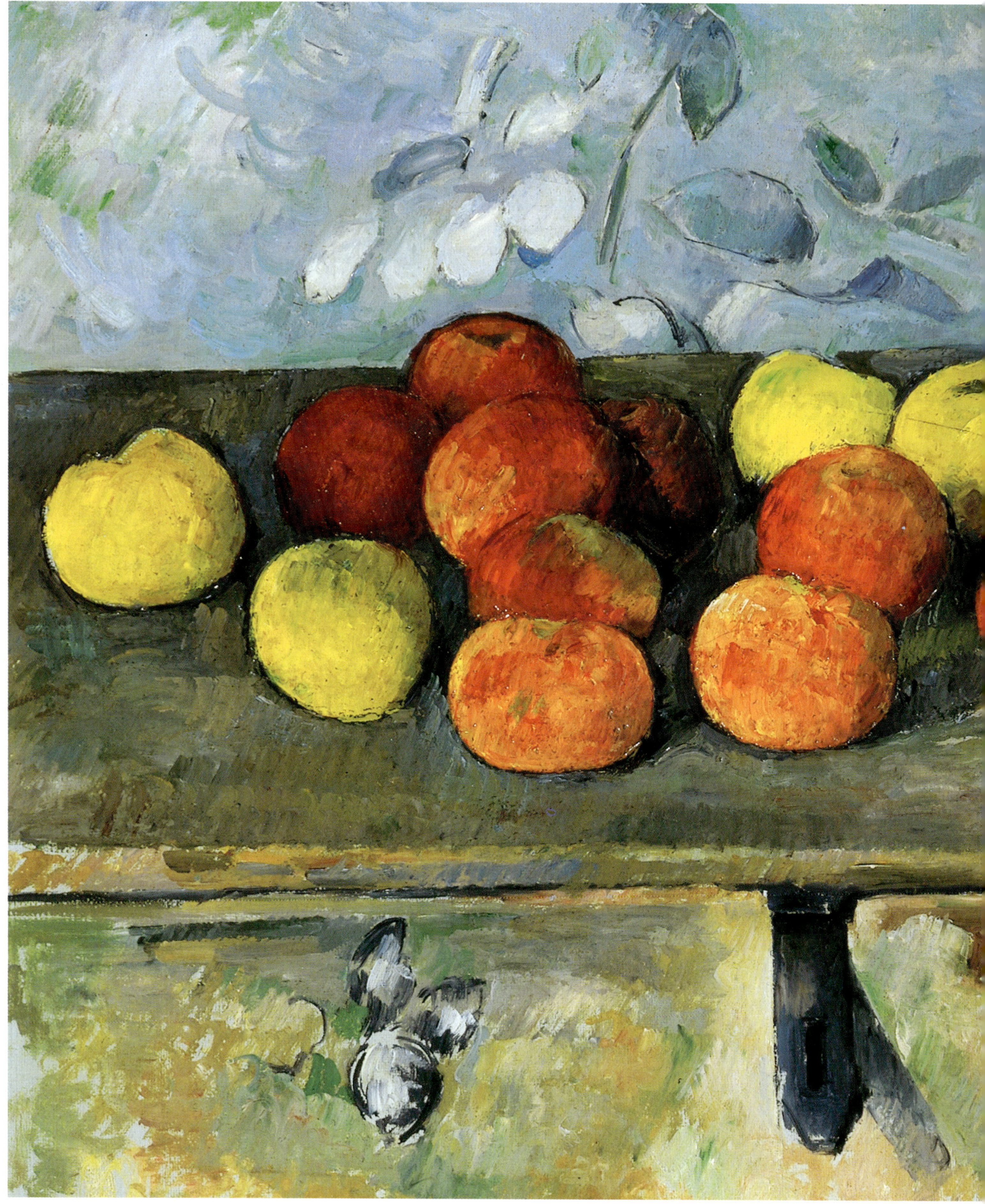

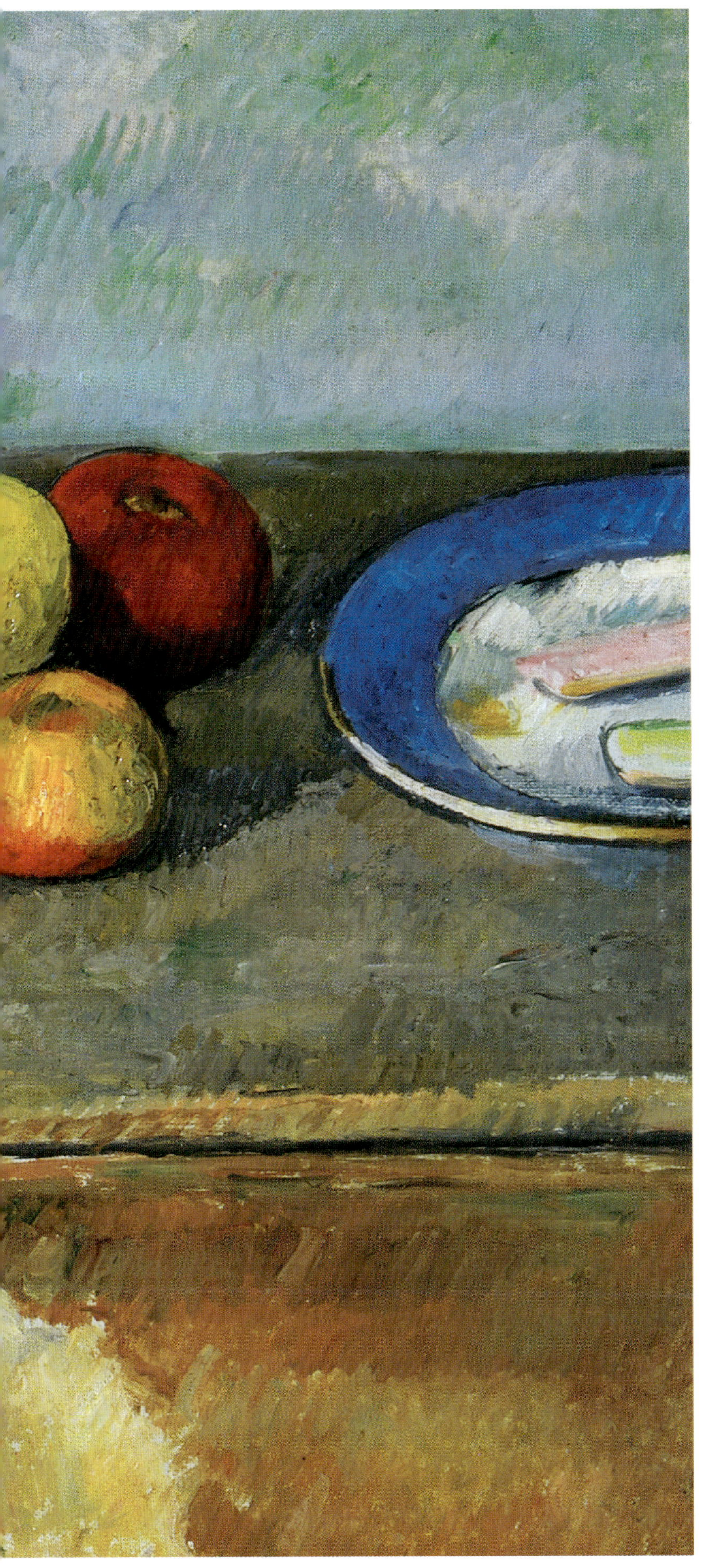

PLATE 16

Still-Life with Apples and Biscuits

(c.1877–80)

Oil on canvas, 15 x 21²/₃ inches (38 x 55cm)

This careful composition, divided horizontally into three near equal bands of different tonal values (the lowest in the centre) is contrived to establish a calm balance of simple elements within the central band, only enlivened by the harsh darks in the lower and the delicate shapes in the upper. It is a subject that Cézanne repeats a number of times around the end of the 1870s. One critic wrote: ' ...this still-life is among the purest of Cézanne's maturity, one of those that best sums up the essential characteristics of his art in his most serene period.' The calm presentation of these unimportant objects gives them a quality of inevitability, the sense of complete harmony for which Cézanne was always searching.

PLATE 17

Still-Life with Apples and Biscuits (c.1880)

overleaf

Oil on canvas, 18 x 21²/₃ inches (46 x 55cm)

A comparison with the previous illustration will indicate where Cézanne's interest lies. It is not in the objects depicted, nor their disposition on the surface, but lies in a determination to discover an immanent relationship in the area of the canvas and his vision of it as a captured harmony. He has three bands again, but of different proportions, which lay emphasis on the central white cloth which supports the apples. He has introduced a dynamic relationship in the opposition of the circular apples and the star decorations of the wallpaper, while a solid band of deep-red apples balances the dancing lighter ones.

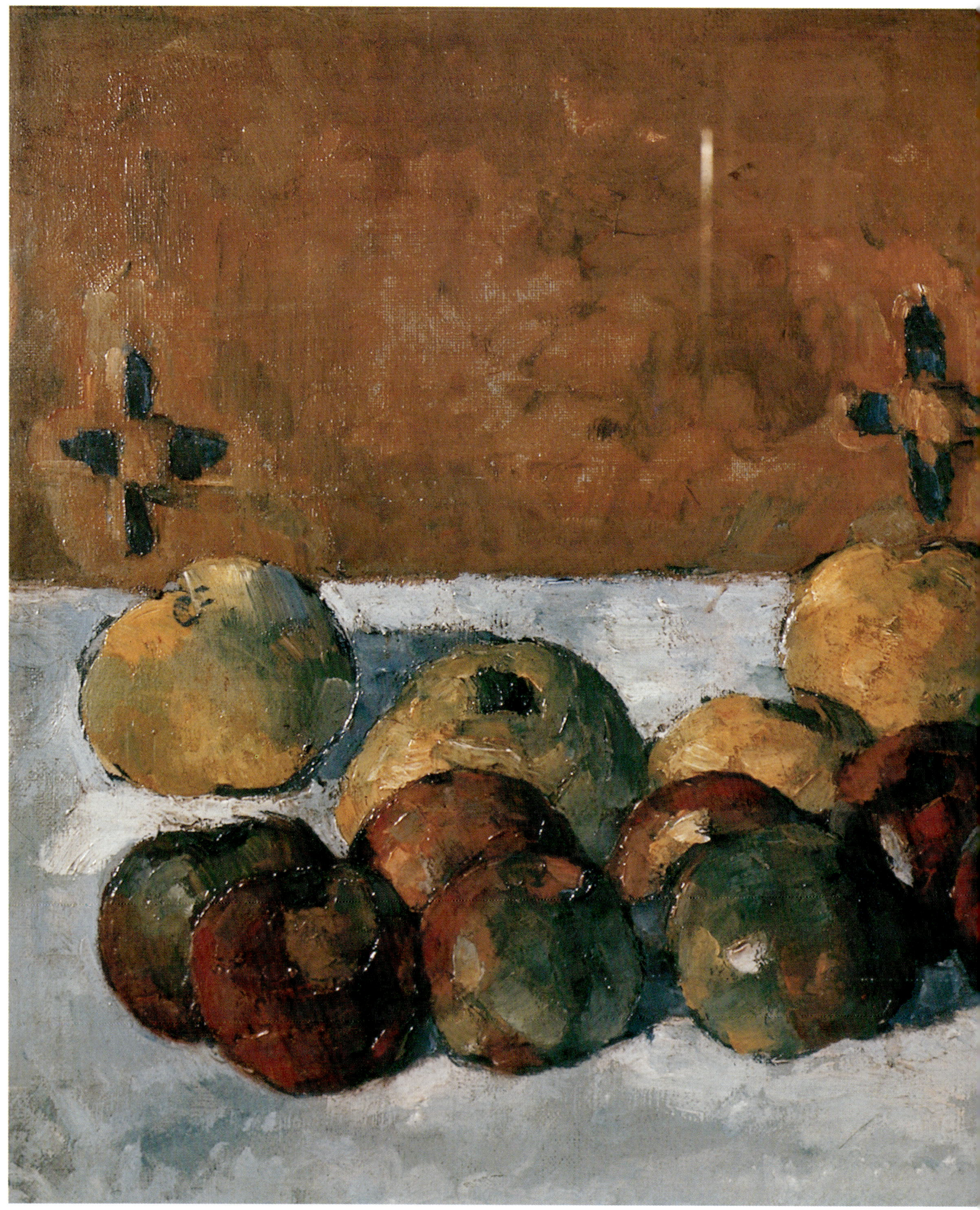

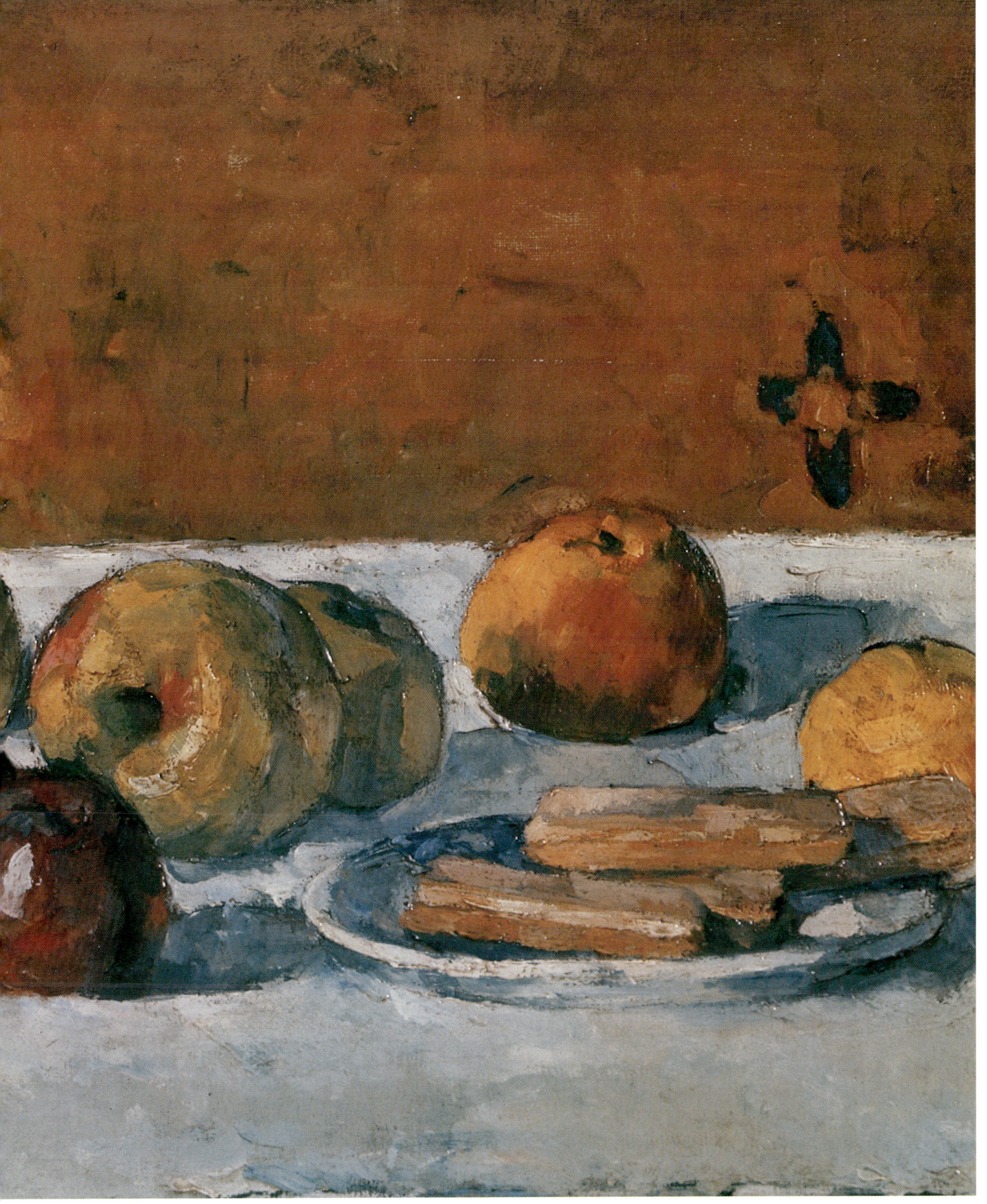

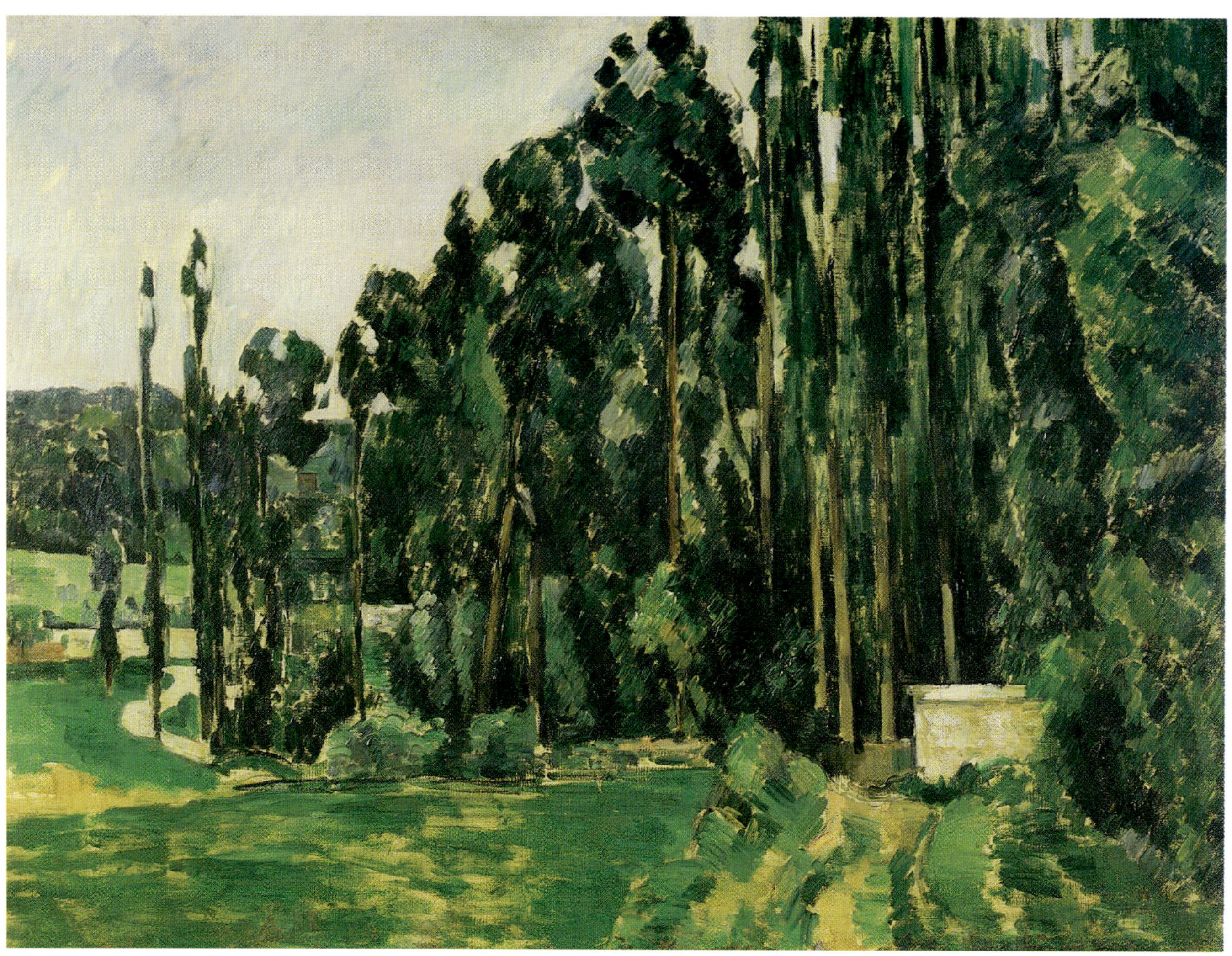

Continued from page 26

with large red eyeballs standing out from his head in a most ferocious manner' as her first impression, she goes on to admit that she had misjudged him by his appearance since he had, in fact, 'the gentlest manner possible, *comme un enfant*'. She was startled by his table manners: he scraped his soup plate and poured the dregs into his spoon and tore the meat from his chop with his fingers. Cézanne was also sensitive to what he regarded as a slight or ridicule and his visit to Giverny ended abruptly in the middle of a meal when he suspected his friends, who had actually been making complimentary remarks about his work, were laughing at him. He returned immediately to Aix without even informing Monet, who nevertheless returned several canvases that Cézanne had left at the hotel in his haste. They never met again. A further indication of Cézanne's provincial small-town attitude is revealed in his first meeting with Rodin when he knelt to kiss Rodin's hand, not because he was a great sculptor but because he had been awarded the Légion d'Honneur.

In the following year, Ambroise Vollard, the dealer

PLATE 18

Poplars (1879–82)

Oil on canvas, $25^1/_2$ x $31^7/_8$ inches (65 x 81cm)

The sensation of poplars is, as Monet too has demonstrated, their verticality and in the mass they produce a green density, punctuated by thin lines which are vertical, or nearly so. Cézanne's development, by about 1880, had introduced what became a characteristic and identifying means of applying paint in parallel brushstrokes. He has used the verticals, as he usually does, as stabilizing elements in a combination with parallel brushstrokes in opposing directional blocks. The two slim trees on the left edge are the spatially defining elements against the curving path, giving an overall effect of a rich and verdant landscape. The location has been identified as just north of Pontoise where Cézanne had been living at the time.

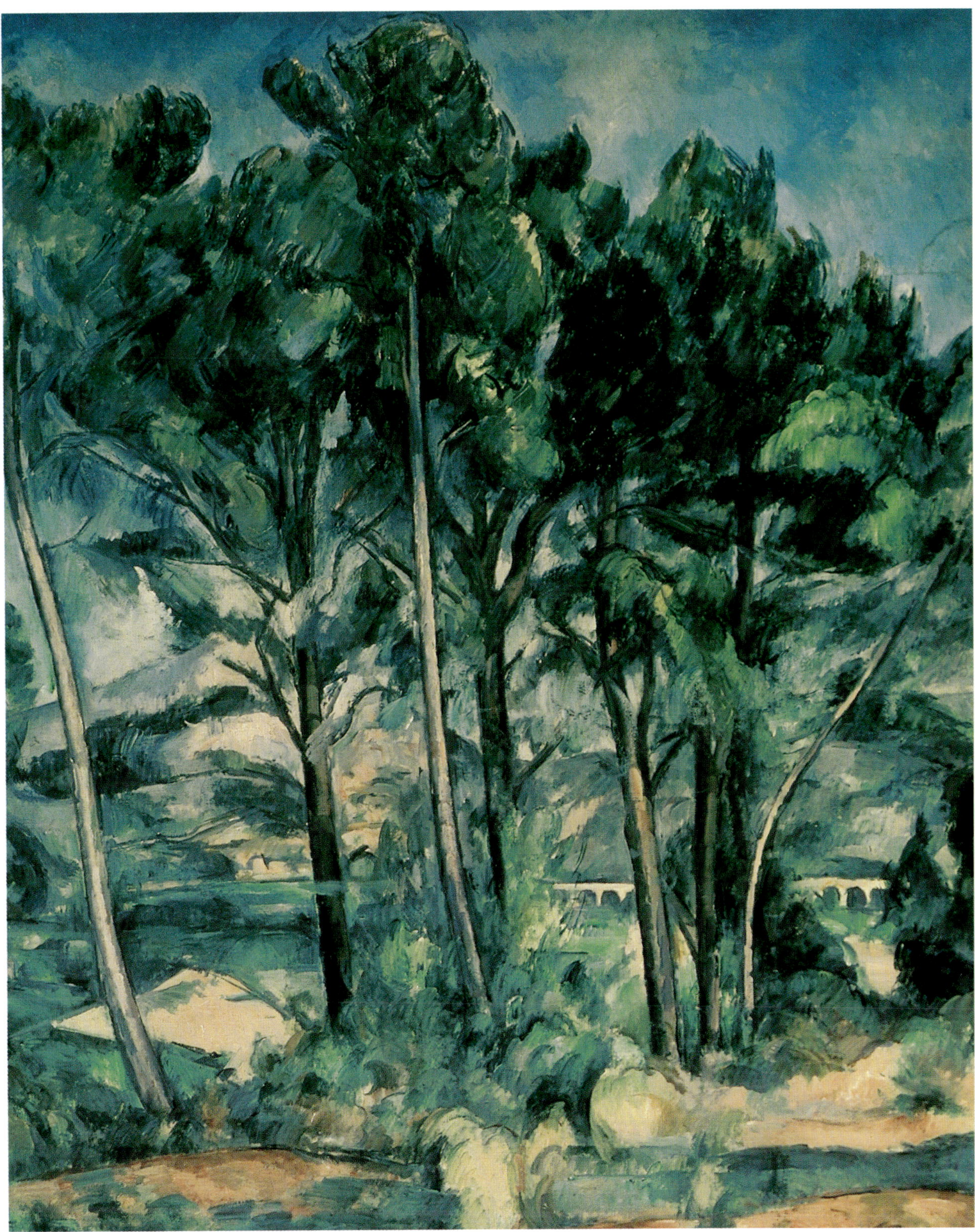

PLATE 19

The Aqueduct (1885–87) detail

Oil on canvas, $35^{3}/_{4}$ x $28^{1}/_{3}$ inches (91 x 72cm)

The aqueduct in the Arc valley below Mont Sainte-Victoire appears in many of Cézanne's paintings, executed when he was in Aix. One of his vantage points was the farm owned by his sister, Rose, and it is from here that most of the famous paintings of Mont Sainte-Victoire, now one of the most familiar views in Western painting, were produced. In this painting, the so-called aqueduct provides the stabilizing horizontal in the painting of trees near Bellevue. The extraordinary vitality of the tree-trunks invests the whole painting with a life that is essentially pictorial, that is to say internal.

PLATE 20

Still-Life with Fruits, Napkin and Milk Jug

(c. 1879–82)

Oil on canvas, $23^{2}/_{3}$ x $28^{1}/_{3}$ inches (60 x 72cm)

Painted in the location of the still-life in plate 17, this composition is almost equally and horizontally divided, but it will be noticed that a curious 'inaccuracy' has been introduced. The far edge to the left of the napkin does not follow the line of the rear edge on the right. Some explanation of this seems necessary: the suggestion of incompetence that may immediately come to mind cannot be sustained when Cézanne's concern with the total picture area is recalled. Why then? – if one also recalls that Cézanne is searching always for a unity and harmony, not the simple reproduction of the scene. If one considers moving the rear-edge line either up or down, one realizes that the delicate balance of the structure of relationships would fall apart; the milk jug would lose its identity, for instance. It is a major part of Cézanne's significance for later painters that he is creating a non-adjustable pictorial object.

that supported him, organized his first exhibition of Cézanne's work, having been encouraged to do so by Pissarro; Cézanne showed 150 paintings – a fair indication of his dedication to his art since he was a slow worker. An example of this is revealed in a reported conversation between them while Vollard was being painted by Cézanne. After 115 sittings, Vollard, not unnaturally perhaps, enquired how the painting was progressing and Cézanne replied, 'I am not displeased with the shirt front.' (See plate 41.) This remains not only an indication of Cézanne's way of working but the seriousness of the reply is a clue to his character.

Gustave Caillebotte, a painter and collector who had died two years earlier, had made a great collection of paintings including Impressionist works, and had left it to the State. Renoir was his executor and had some trouble persuading the authorities to accept the legacy. Ultimately, in 1895, 65 of the works came to the national collection. Of the five by Cézanne, only two were accepted by the directors and entered the Luxembourg Museum collection. Later, Vollard bought the entire collection of work in one of Cézanne's studios. It had been a slow progress and Cézanne was by no means universally admired or widely understood but by the end of the century he was recognized by many as a master, a fact evidenced by the painting *Hommage à Cézanne* which Maurice Denis, a

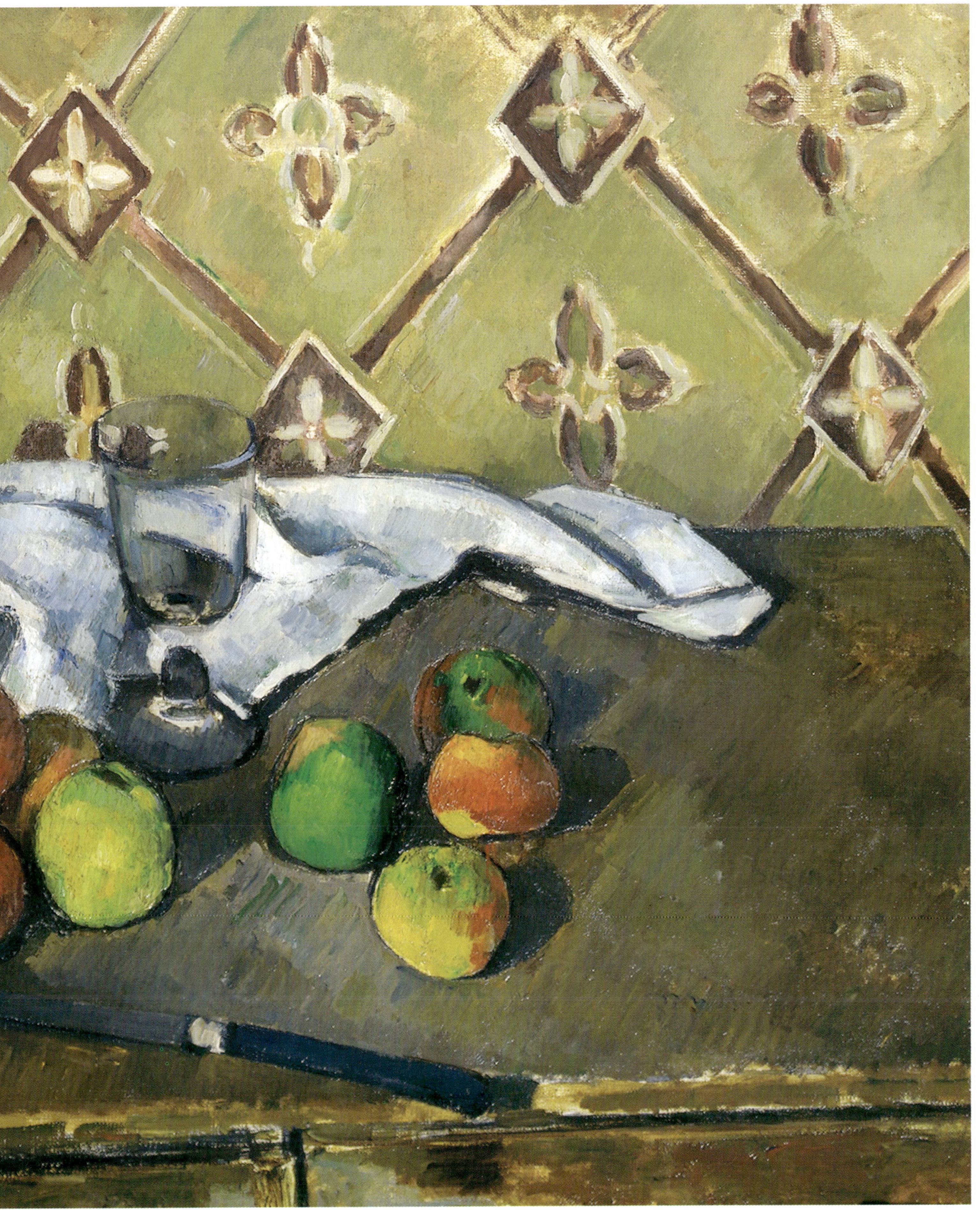

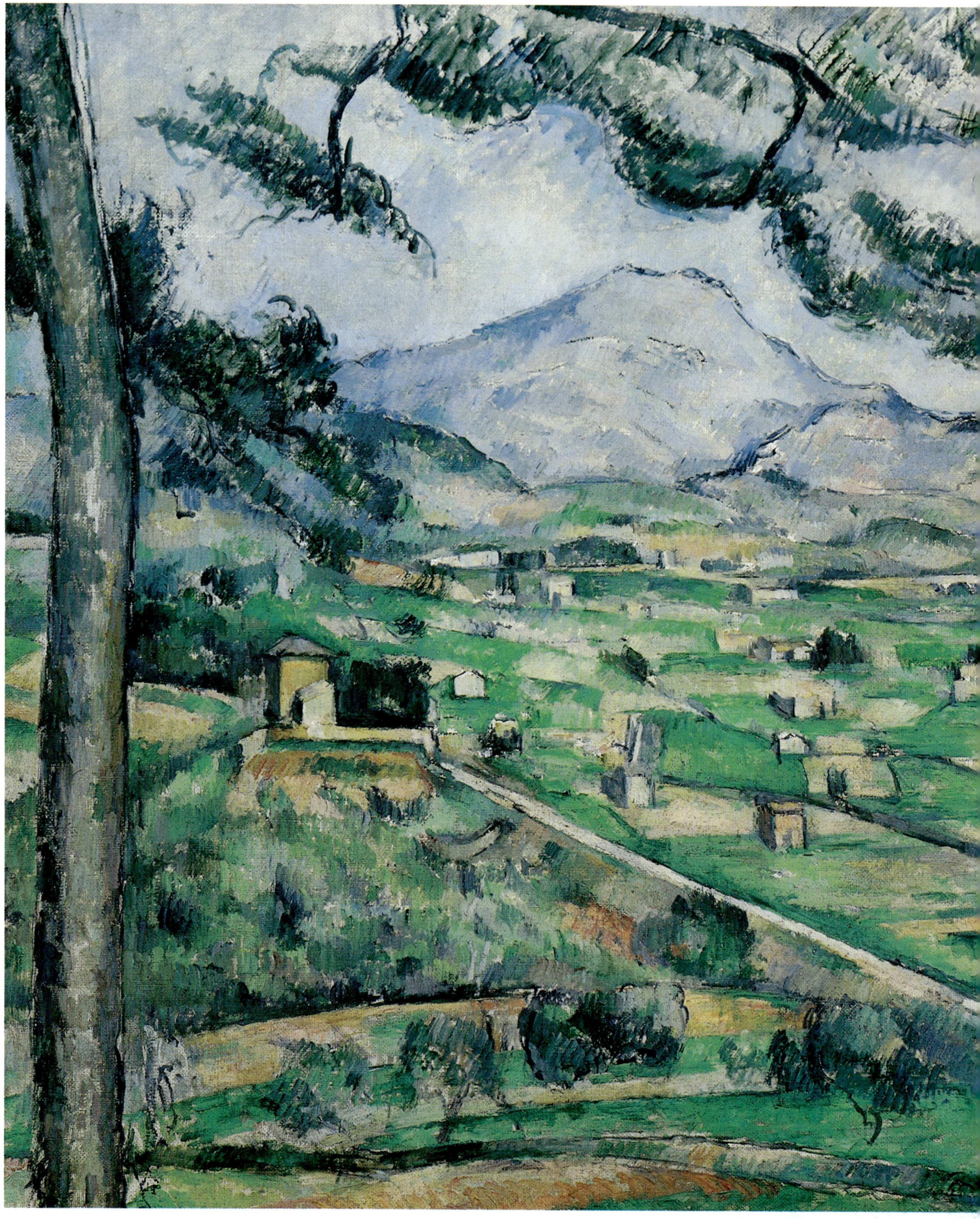

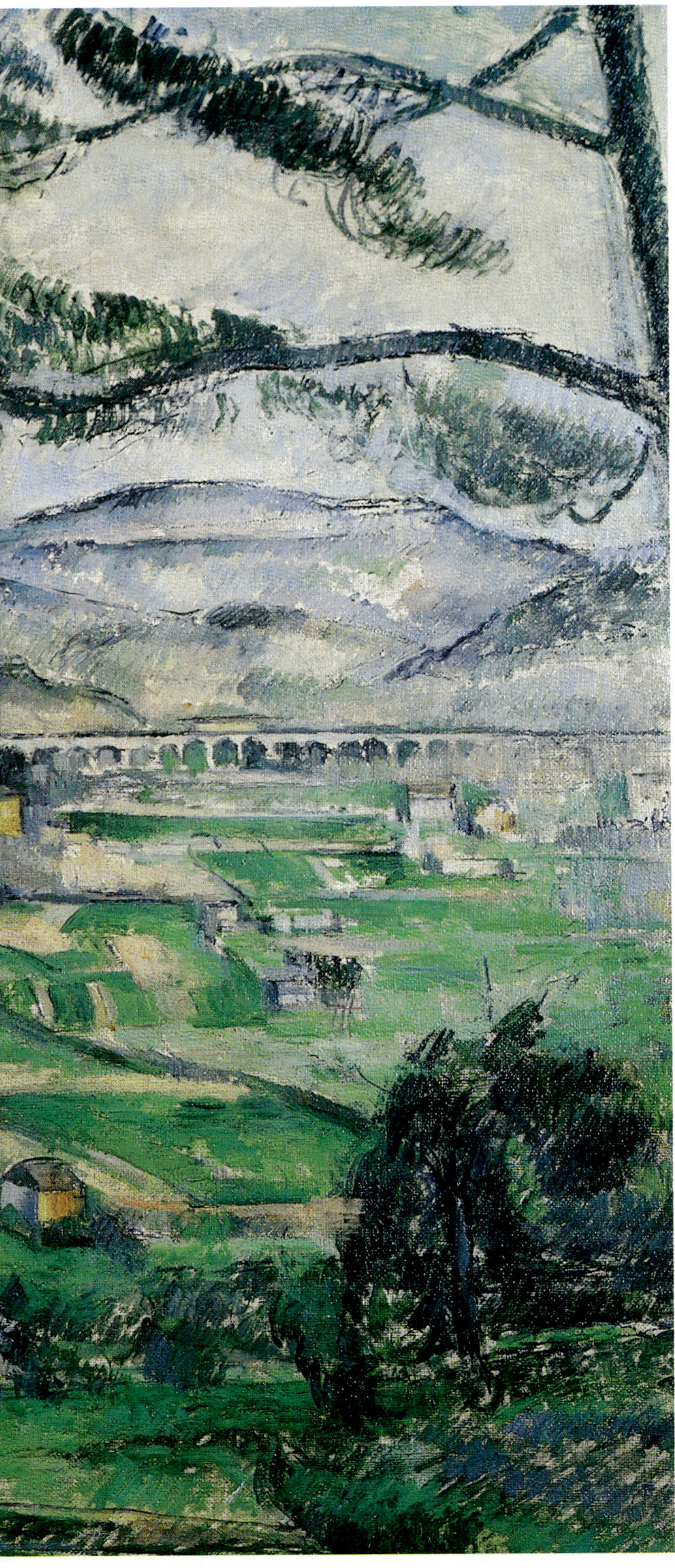

PLATE 21

Mont Sainte-Victoire with Large Pine

(1886–87)

Oil on canvas, $23^1/_2$ x $28^1/_2$ inches (59.7 x 72.5cm)

From this same location near the farm Bellevue, Cézanne painted most of his grand views of the mountain that dominated the scene and occupied his mind through the 1880s. What may be declared, however, is that the paintings of this subject produced during the 1880s are part of the most mature and inspiring of what is called his 'classical' period and carry the same authority as great masterpieces from such painters as Poussin. The scene itself is interesting. Cézanne's raised view from Bellevue is across the valley of the river Arc (on the banks of which Cézanne and Zola played as children) to the dominating Mont Sainte-Victoire, named, it is said, in honour of a victory by the Romans over the barbarians in the first century A.D. From his vantage point, the plain stretches uninterrupted to the mountain providing Cézanne with the sort of pictorial problem which would have engaged and delighted him. He was concerned with two things which he described as his motif *and his* petite sensation. *The* motif *was the identity of the subject; the* petite sensation *was its individual special quality. While admitting that this is a simplification of what Cézanne would also call a process of 'logic', it does perhaps indicate that the result would, if successful, be a simple pictorial statement in only its own terms. It is, incidentally, another example of a landscape bisected by a rail line of which the viaduct is the evident reminder. For the Impressionist painters, the train and its implications was a symbol of the impact of modern life upon the historic landscape, evidence of which is seen in the work of Monet, Renoir, Pissarro, Degas, as well as Cézanne.*

(See also plates 42, 43 and 44.)

PLATE 22

The Bay of Marseille seen from L'Estaque

(1882–85)

Oil on canvas, $22^{3}/_{4}$ x $28^{1}/_{3}$ inches (58 x 72cm)

Cézanne painted this subject a number of times from different viewpoints, some more distant, giving emphasis to the vertical smoke tower seen here in the foreground. He was particularly attracted by the strength in the middle-distance of the bay itself, a flat area of colour in the middle of the picture area with strong forms in the far distance and foreground. Although at first examination this painting may suggest that it is Impressionist in character, it is actually more in keeping with the investigations that Cézanne was making into pictorial identity and the sea area enables him to construct his 'flat' space above and below to connect the picture plane. It shows an assurance in structured composition of his later work. The painting of the hills and shore in the background is particularly effective when one recalls how a photograph of a distant range of hills appears as a very small area while making a powerful visual impact.

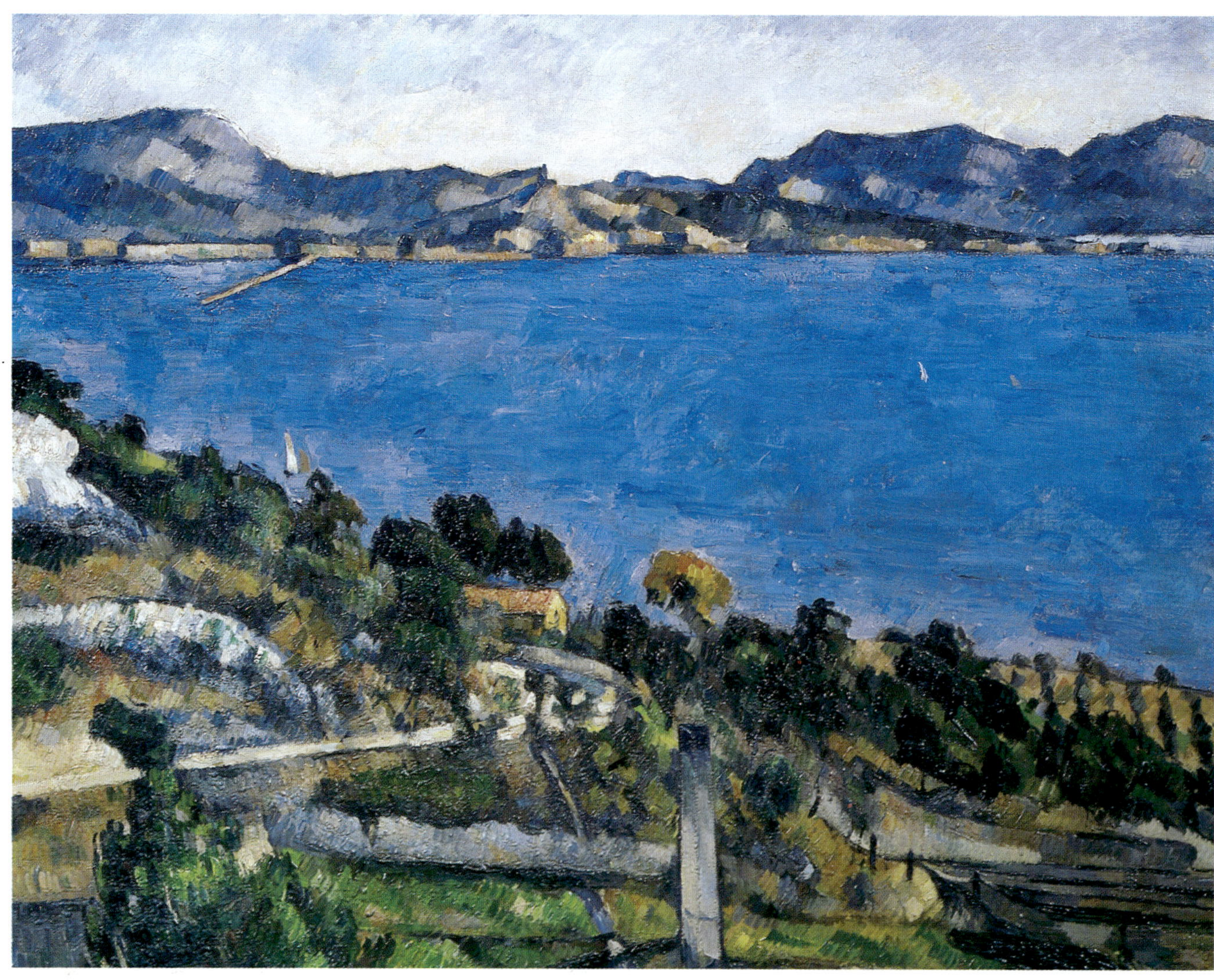

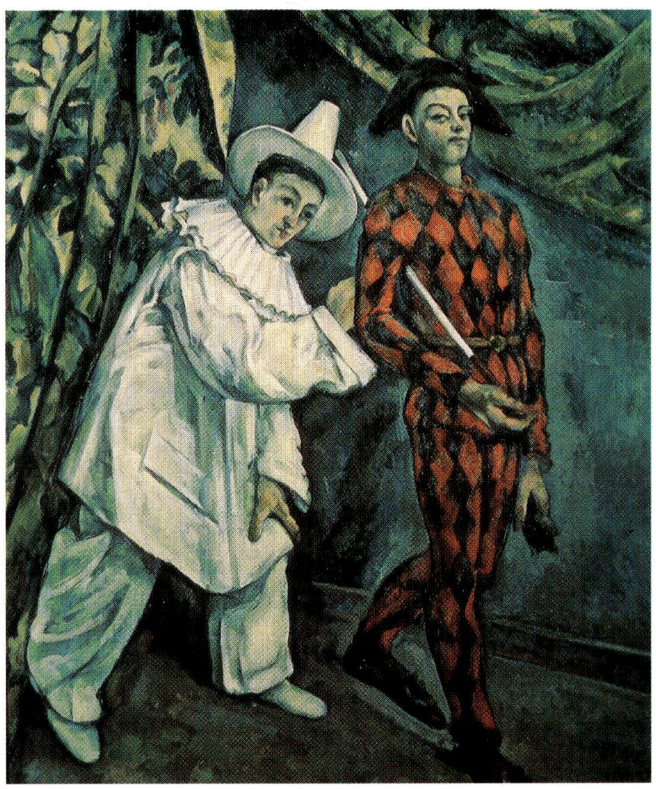

PLATE 23

Pierrot and Harlequin (1888)

Oil on canvas, $40^{1}/_{4}$ x $31^{7}/_{8}$ inches (102 x 81cm)

Also called 'Mardi Gras', this is an unusual painting in the Cézanne oeuvre. *Cézanne made a number of studies for it and a painting of the Harlequin figure alone, but it did not presage a series. According to Paul, Cézanne's son, he posed for the Harlequin figure and his great friend Louis Guillaume, son of a cobbler, for Pierrot. At the time, Paul was 16 and if the story is true he seems to have been a singularly self-assured youth. They are in* commedia dell'arte *costume and it is interesting to note that other painters subsequently chose similar subjects, including Picasso. Cézanne was in Paris when the work was painted and had inherited from his father's estate, giving him a financial freedom which opened up new possibilities, including the ability to pay for professional models. It is also apparent that he had acquired a new interest in the figure and portraiture after many years of concentrating on landscapes and still-lifes.*

member of the Nabis group, exhibited at the Salon of 1901. In 1899 Jas de Bouffan was sold to settle the family estate on the death of Cézanne's mother, and although he had attempted to buy the Château Noir where he had been painting, he failed and worked in various rented premises until 1902 when he moved to the new studio he had built on the Chemin des Lauves at Aix.

In 1902 Émile Bernard published a pamphlet on Cézanne. Zola died in September of the same year, unreconciled with Cézanne who was nevertheless deeply upset and Vollard reports Cézanne weeping at the mention of Zola's name. Pissarro followed in 1903, a close friend to the last. (Cézanne later described himself, in the catalogue of an exhibition in 1906, as a 'pupil of Pissarro'.) In October 1904 at the Second Salon d'Automne in Paris, an entire room containing 31 paintings and two drawings was devoted to Cézanne's work and he is listed as one of the Salon's founding members. Moreover, in October 1906, another ten Cézannes were included in the famous Salon d'Automne which included the work of the Fauve painters, Matisse, Derain and Vlaminck, members of the first of the 20th-century art movements and which reflected the influence of Cézanne. He himself was by that time seriously ill.

The summer had been very hot and Cézanne had been working in the open-air from dawn while ill with diabetes and undergoing what he describes as an 'atrocious' course of treatment, including massage from his gardener Vallier. By August he was suffering from an attack of bronchitis but continued working through August and September and into the next month until, on 15 October he collapsed, remaining in the rain for several hours before being brought back on a laundry cart. Despite his, by then, evidently critical condition, he worked the next day in his studio on a portrait of Vallier. His condition deteriorated and five days later on the 22 October 1906 he died. In the exhibition in Aix-en-Provence when he describes himself as a pupil of Pissarro, he was showing the first and last of his works in his birthplace. The painting of the gardener Vallier, unfinished, was his last work.

THE PAINTINGS

Before considering Cézanne's work, there are some general observations that should be made which are specially, although not uniquely, applicable to him and his work.

It is evident in the work of the Impressionists, and indeed most painters after them in this century, that they were not specifically concerned with representing their subjects to a 'photographic' degree. They assumed an independence which allowed them a selective freedom, a choice of emphasis, a use of colour and way of applying paint which neither finitely identifies the forms of objects nor their local surface colour.

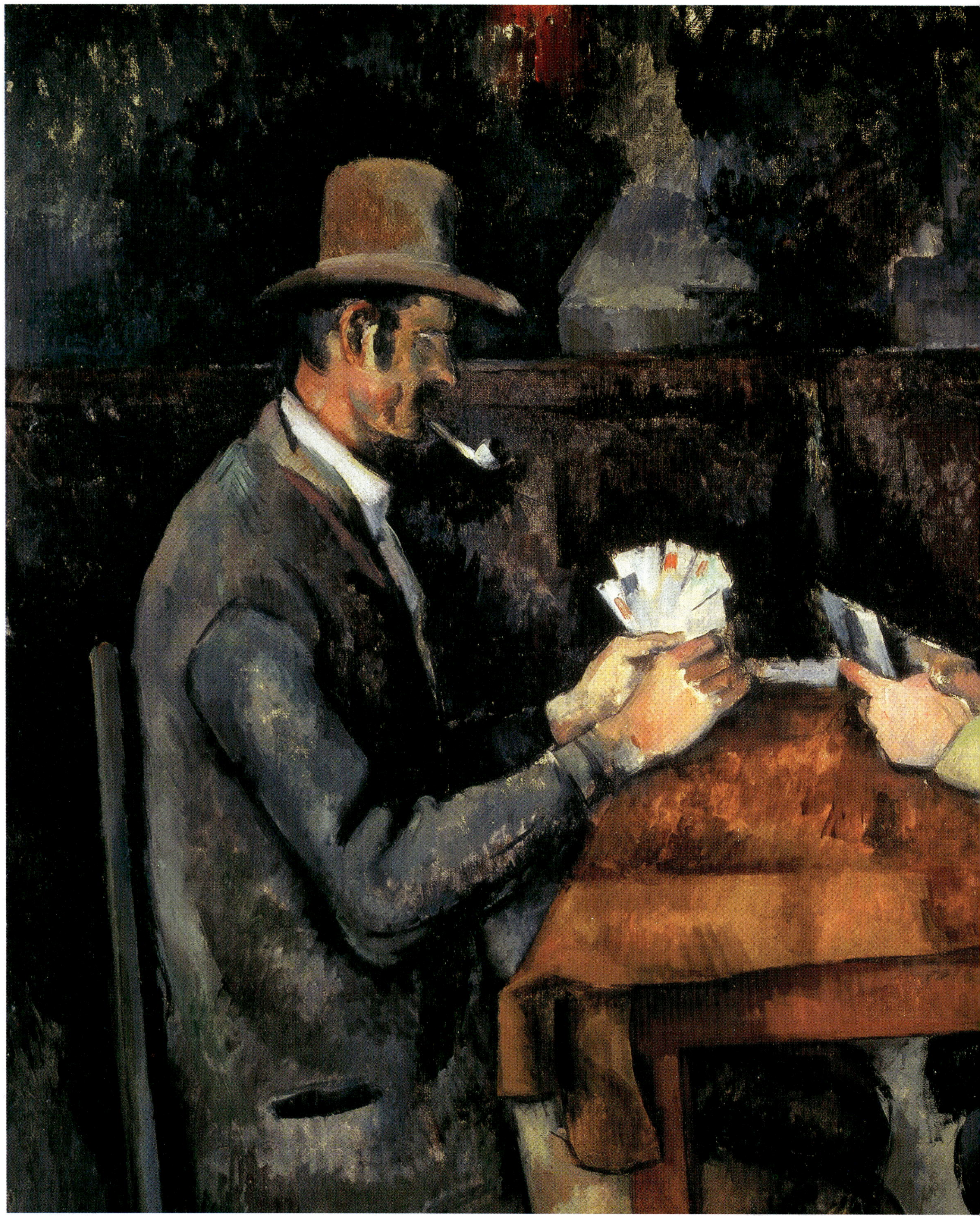

PLATE 24

The Card Players (c. 1893)

Oil on canvas, $17^{3}/_{4}$ x $22^{1}/_{2}$ inches (45 x 57cm)

Cézanne painted a short series of five paintings of this subject, in two of which he included other figures. The main element in these paintings is the relaxed concentration and direct opposition of the two protagonists. Cézanne is not interested in presenting an emotional scene but is attempting to achieve with the balanced interaction of the two central figures a pictorial, tensioned structure. The off-verticals of the table-legs, together with the off-horizontals of the table-top, introduce a tension that also adds to the pictorial structure.

The Impressionists had, to this extent at least, initiated a revolution which in its outcome had a profound effect on attitudes to painting, firstly in France and eventually throughout the world. It was no mean achievement for young painters who were, in the main, still students when the need for urgent changes in painting attitudes and methods began to dominate their thinking. They were not a unified group with set aims and clear direction. They did not think of themselves as Impressionists – some in fact never did – but they did wish to be independent enough to paint as they felt. This was not what they were being taught, nor what they saw in exhibitions or at the Salon to which all professional painters wished to submit their work and have it shown. Salon works were linked indissolubly to the historical tradition of both technique and subject. The technique was tied to the Renaissance-defined, if also refined and subtle, representation of form through line or edge. The areas within were identified with a local colour, the colour of the subject (whether a body or some object) being modified by the addition of lighter or darker tone to identify volume. This admittedly simplistic description of what became, in the hands of the great painters and even able practitioners, a technique of almost unlimited flexibility and variety during the later 17th and 18th centuries (in the later years of the 18th century and early 19th it became the style known as Neo-Classicism), turned again to defined form and local colour which became the

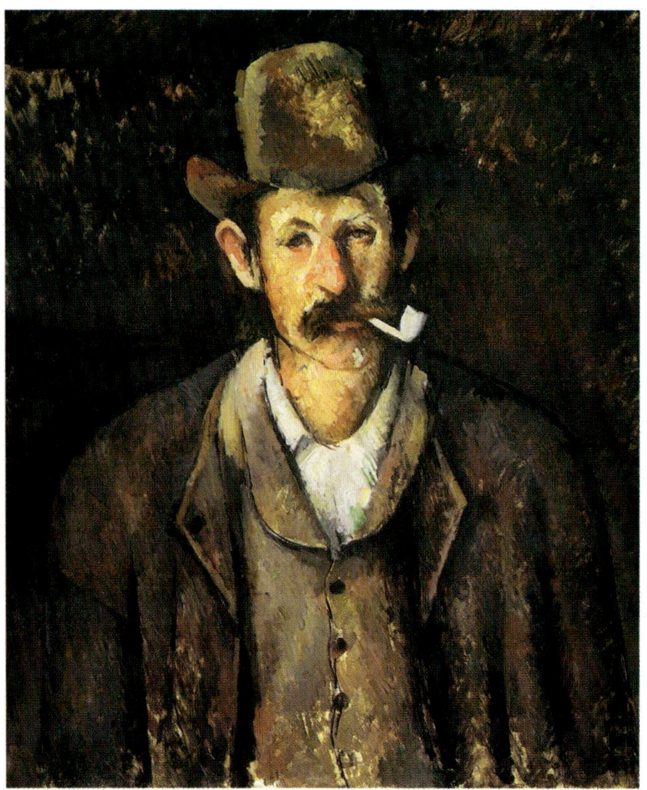

PLATE 25
Man Smoking a Pipe (c. 1892)
Oil on canvas, $28^{3}/_{4}$ x $23^{2}/_{3}$ inches (73 x 60cm)

The subject of this work is the same person who appears as the figure on the left in The Card Players *in plate 24. He was Cézanne's gardener, Vallier, who was also the subject of the last painting Cézanne was working on when he died. This is one of the portraits that he painted in the late 1880s and early 1890s. Like many of his works, particularly of this period, the painting is unfinished in that small areas of the canvas have been left uncovered. Despite this, the work seems complete in its statement and this is a reminder that Cézanne insisted that each small stroke was significant and until he could identify what it should be he could not place it in the painting. (For an elaboration of this point, see the note to his portrait of Ambroise Vollard, his dealer and friend, in plate 41.)*

standard practice for Salon work.

The subject-matter was also clearly identified in the Salon. The 'important' works were of an intellectually 'elevated' character, dealing with significant historical or religious subjects designed for an 'educated' taste. A nude was not a nude but a Venus or Hercules. Landscapes were admitted and, although still-life paintings were accepted, they were not considered of the highest order and were required to be of a traditional character and technique.

The young independents found these limitations unacceptable and looked for alternatives. They found them in the work of Courbet, the Barbizon painters and Delacroix. An adequate consideration of their work is not possible within the limited space available here, but it is important to recognize that each was outside the academic tradition; the Barbizan painters, deeply enamoured with the local landscape around the Forest of Fontainebleau, and painting in the open-air; Courbet concerned with the dignity and poverty of the peasant life of his village, Ornans; Delacroix, the great figure of the Romantic opposition to Classicism and a painter whose attitude, painting technique and different subject-matter had the greatest impact on the young independent painters. One of his subjects *Women of Algiers* was much admired by the young painters and is a romantic parallel to Ingres' 'Turkish harem'.

By the 1860s, the conditions for an artistic revolution

PLATE 26
The Smoker (c. 1892)
Oil on canvas, $36^{1}/_{4}$ x $28^{3}/_{4}$ inches (92 x 73cm)

The sitter appears in the Card Players series and has been identified as a labourer who worked at Jas de Bouffan called Alexandre Paullin. He is depicted in the kitchen or studio of the house with his elbow on what appears to be either the top of a ribbed chest or a patterned tablecloth. To the left, there is a grey flue pipe which holds the left side and concentrates the composition on the head, arm and strong worker's hand. The sitter seems relaxed and is quizzically regarding the artist and viewer, certainly a far cry from art critic Louis Vauxcelle's comment that Cézanne painted 'the heads of shifty obstinate peasants'. Cezanne made a preparatory drawing showing the man leaning on a table-top and it seems that Cézanne changed his intention in this area, as a line continuing the table-top can be discerned in the painting. The drawing was once in the possession of Gertrude Stein, in Paris, and it is more than probable that her artist friends, which included Matisse and Picasso, would have seen it.

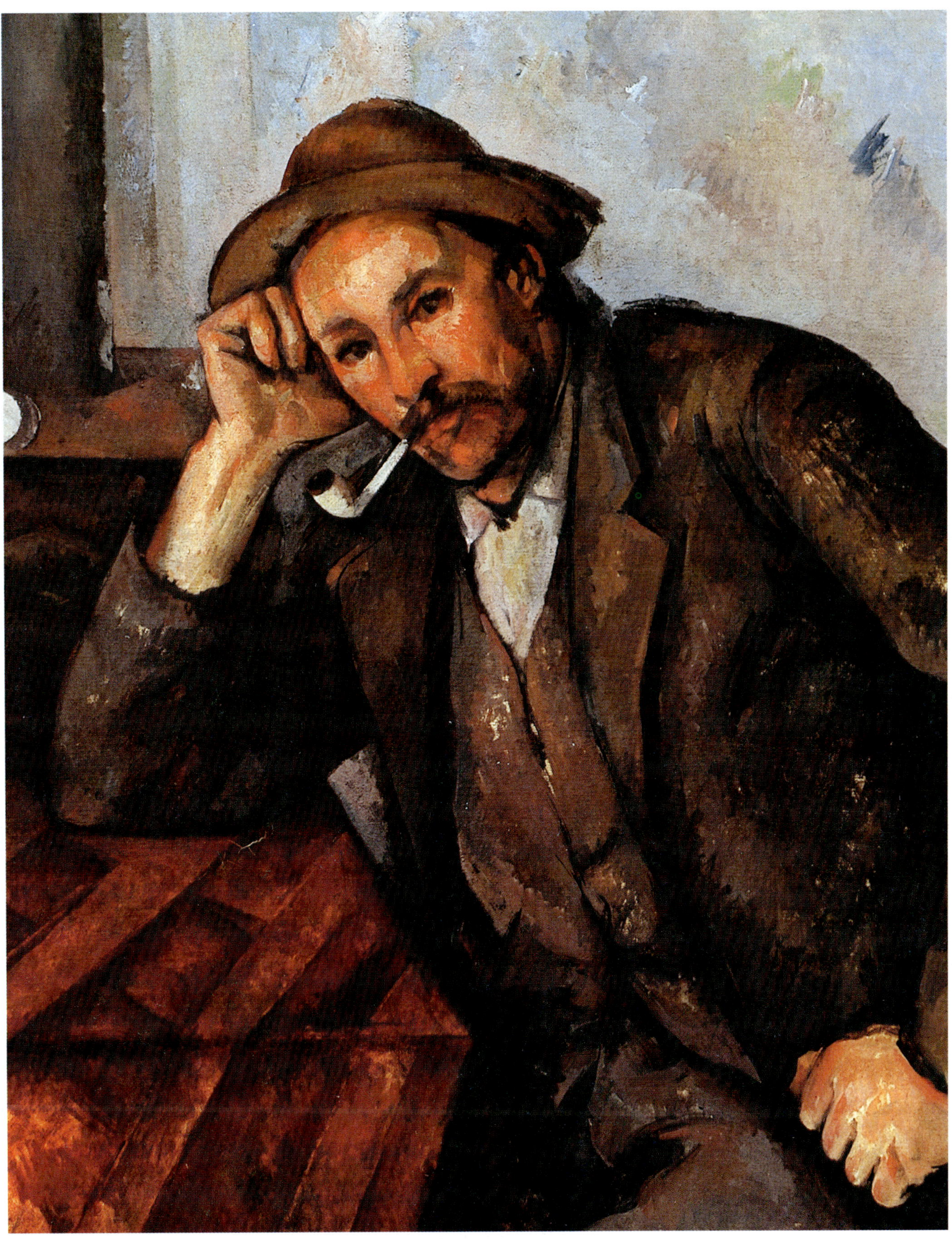

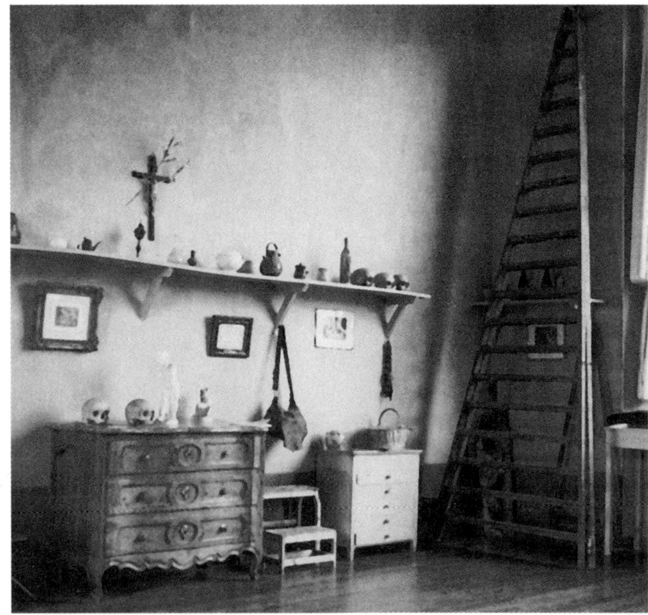

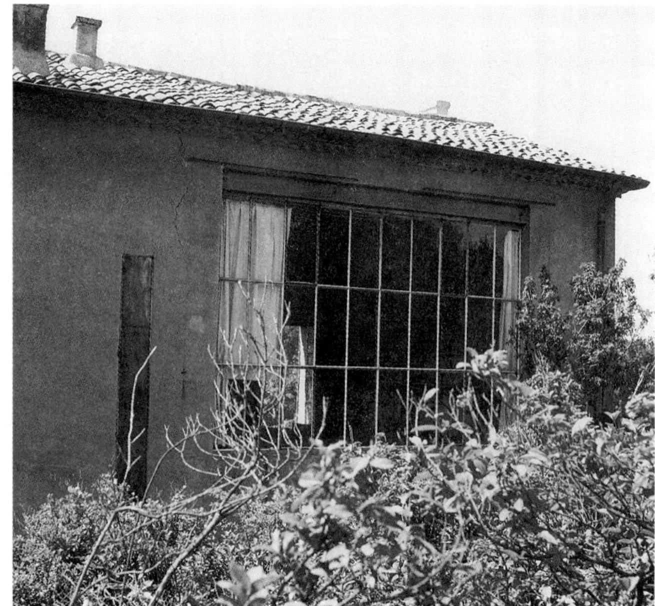

PLATES 27 and 27a above
The interior and exterior of Cézanne's studio in Aix-en-Provence

PLATE 28 opposite
An elderly Cézanne in his studio while working on the *Large Bathers*

existed and were given focus by the paintings of Édouard Manet whose developing technique was of such importance that with two notorious works, *Le déjeuner sur l'herbe* (1863) and *Olympia* (1865) he became the leader, if somewhat reluctantly, of the independents who were to become the Impressionists. He did not, as has been noted, exhibit in their first exhibition in 1874, or in the subsequent seven that took place.

As we have seen in looking at his life, Cézanne was involved with the group and, under the influence of Pissarro, was for a short time associated with Impressionism. His importance is, however, not in his short-lived Impressionist period, but in the work he later produced; it would not be inappropriate to describe it as anti-Impressionist although it is more usually described as Post-Impressionist – accurately because it was later than Impressionism, but unhelpfully since it says nothing about either the quality or nature of his work.

It is perhaps of some value here to remember that life is a process of change, of advance or regression, of heightening sensitivities or stolid contentment, of descent into mediocrity or, for a few, triumphant achievement. What is certain is that humanity does not start at the highest level of accomplishment – it is attained. The artist, in almost every case, progresses from tentative beginnings towards his or her ultimate goal, passing through many stages in the process.

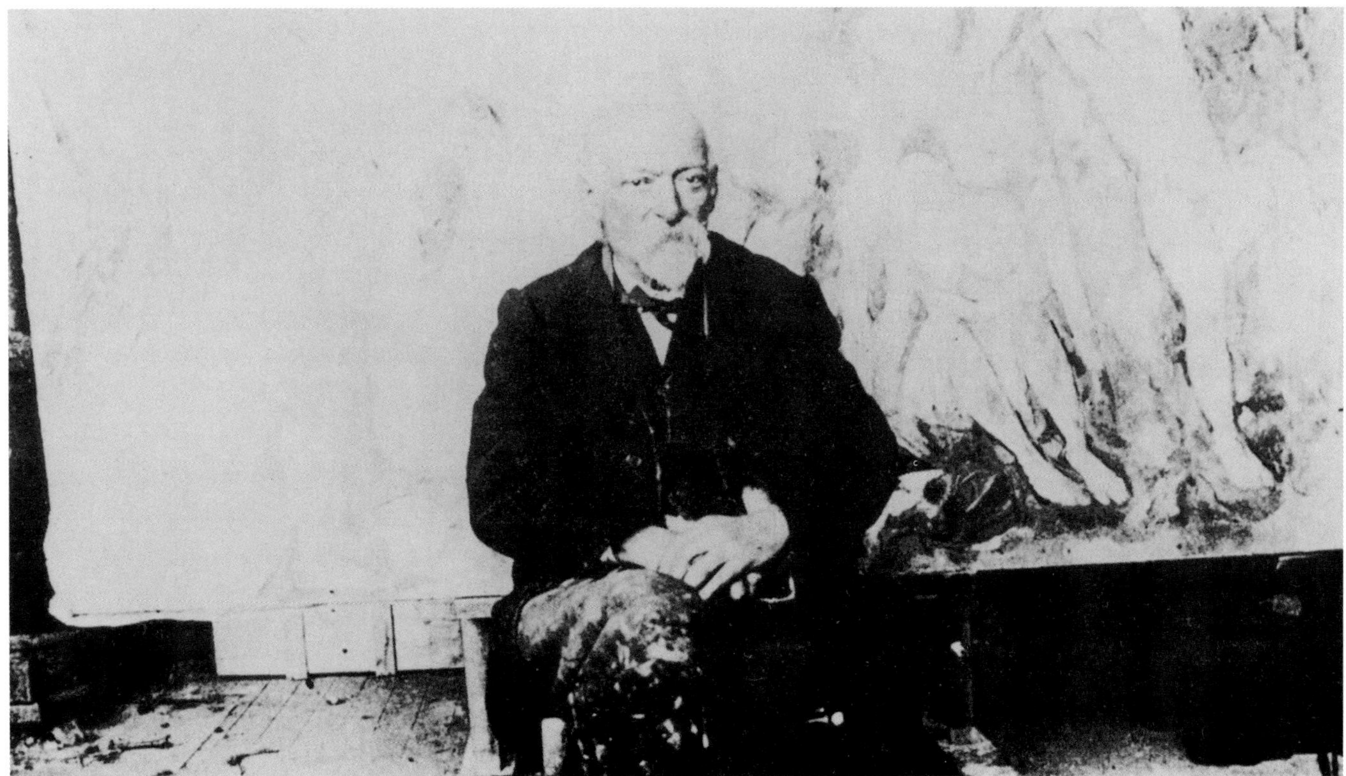

Cézanne's importance lies more in the work produced after the Impressionist phase rather than before or in it. And that achievement is linked more with this century than with the previous one. It is what Cézanne did after Impressionism that constitutes his major importance. It is likely that, had he not come so positively under the influence of Pissarro when he did, he would not have been an Impressionist at all. That is not to diminish Pissarro's importance to Cézanne because Pissarro had an ordered programme and clear ideas concerning the nature of painting that went beyond Impressionism and which were more in keeping with Cézanne's temperament. This is not to claim that Cézanne had a coherent programme although he was both tentative and deliberate as his work developed.

He was dedicated to his work, sensitive, easily offended, protective but unsure of his ideas, convinced of his art and with a belief that it would be eventually recognized – a belief justified in his lifetime. He was fortunate in that, from early in his career, he had supporters – even indeed, when he was an unsuccessful pupil in Aix. It is also important to remind ourselves that although for a time he was confined by a reduced allowance from his father, he was never actually forced to work for a living; painting could and did remain the entire focus of his energies and his later concentration was not distracted by financial worries.

The paintings that Cézanne's name generally recall are not his early works, which are interesting more for their potential than for what they accomplished. At the time, they occasioned pitying rather than vitriolic criticism and it is a measure of the sensitivity of some of his friends and one or two collectors who bought his work that this potential was recognized. He had begun his art studies in Aix without any marked success. He went to the Free Drawing School in 1857 and worked there until he arrived in Paris in 1861 where he met Pissarro and began his professional career. His work at the Free School was undistinguished and academic studies of the nude in pencil show him to have been capable of what most students manage to achieve but usually do not surpass. There are some drawings from the early 1860s which indicate the development of a heavy, coarse drawing style which, during the 1860s, he continued in his early oil paintings. He was probably in Paris throughout the whole of 1863 and exhibited in the Salon des Refusés with Manet's *Déjeuner.* He also studied at the Académie Suisse where, in 1861, he had met Pissarro. During the whole of this period he was working in thick impasto paint, often applied with a palette knife, on subjects ranging from nudes to still-lifes. His *Bread with Eggs* (1865), recalls both the 17th-century Spanish painters and Manet in its dark ground with highlighted objects. In the *Sugar Bowl, Pears and Blue Cup,* painted about the same time, he uses a

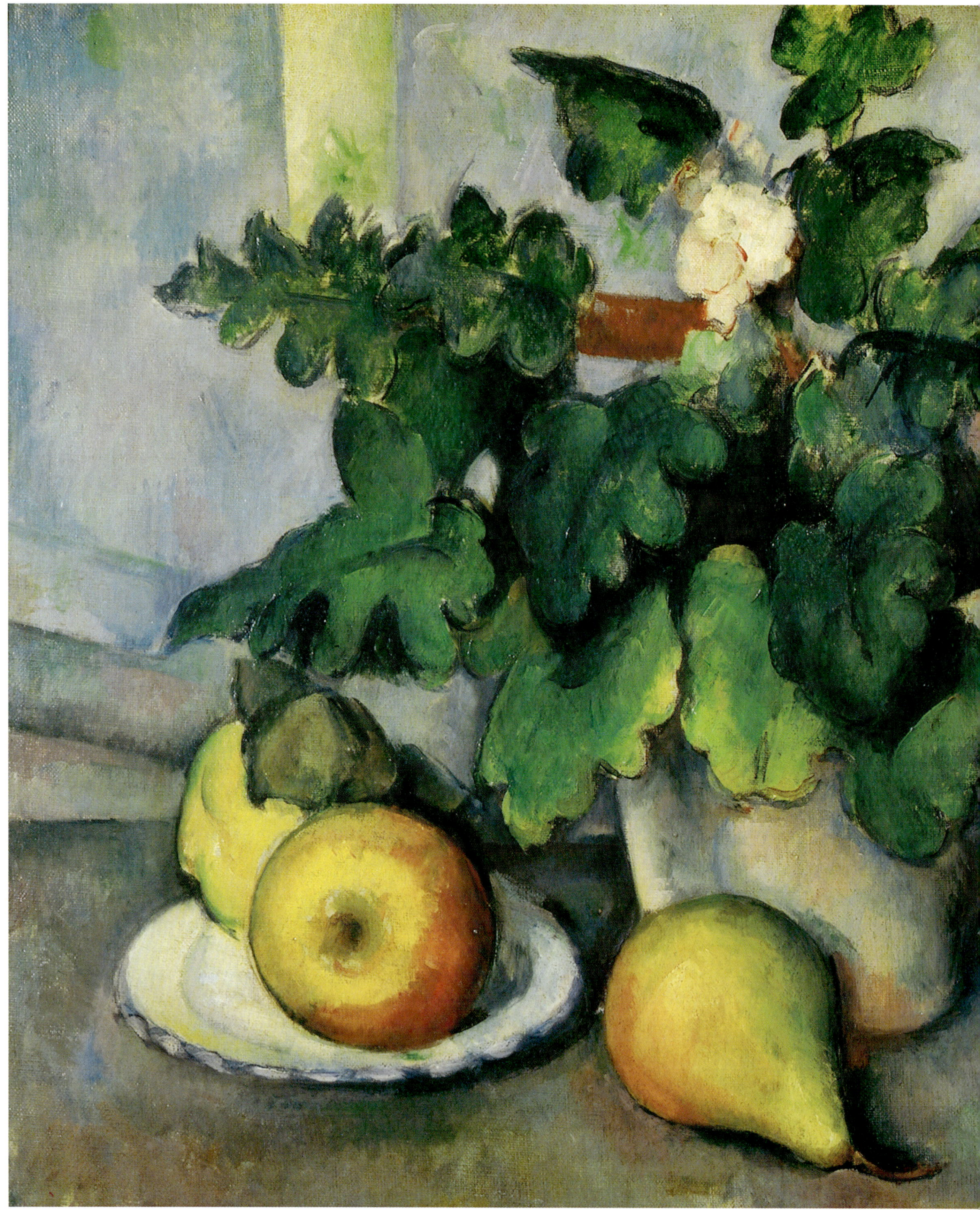

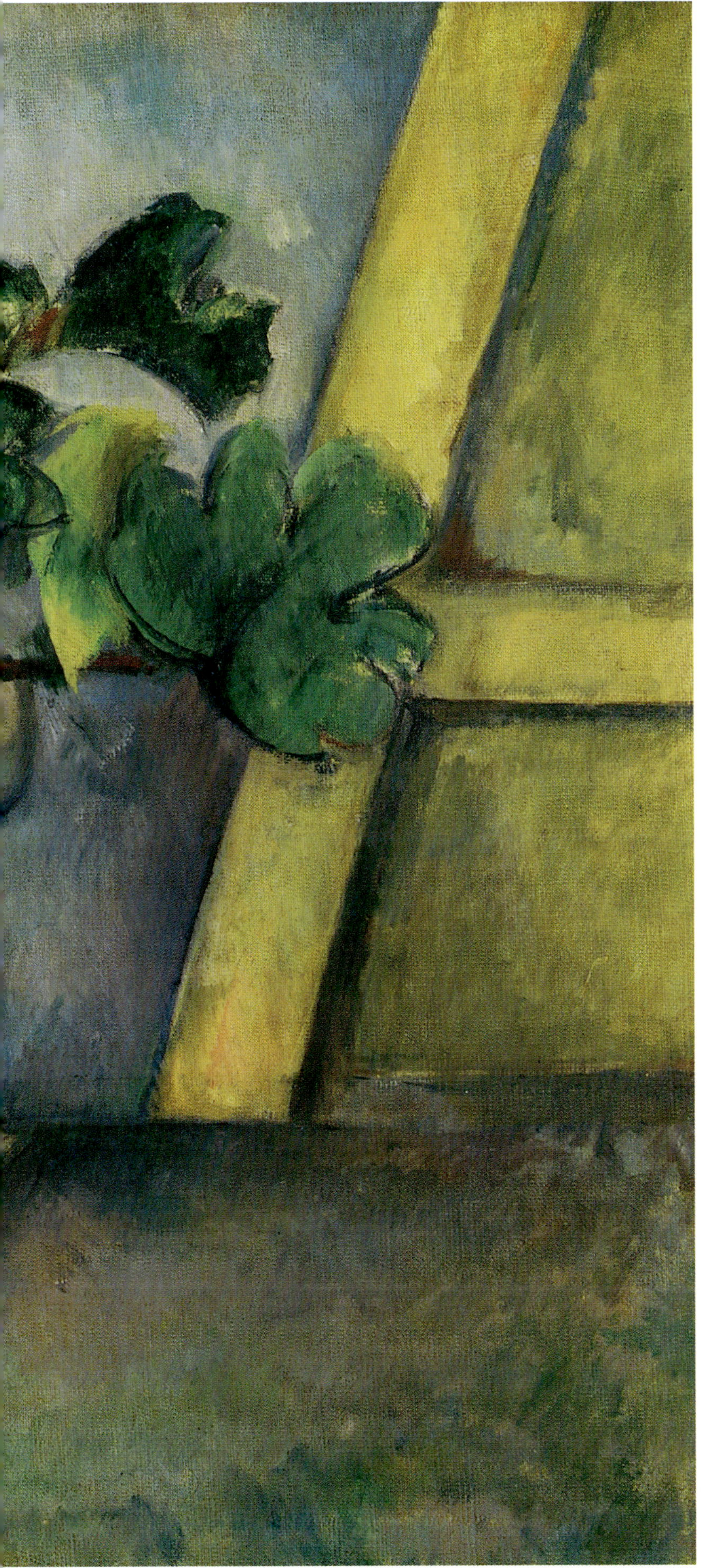

PLATE 29
Still-Life of Pot of Flowers and Pears
(1888–90)
Oil on canvas, $17^{3}/_{4}$ x $21^{1}/_{4}$ inches (45 x 54cm)

In this simple still-life (as in plate 20), the far edge of the table-top is at different heights as it passes behind the objects and indeed the angle on the far right is steeper than on the left. Degas in his paintings of women bathing used the same steep perspective to draw the viewer into the painted scene. It is clear that Cézanne wanted to unify the table-top with the slanting canvas behind. It is this flattening distortion that the Cubists were later to exploit. There is a well known comment by Kandinsky in his seminal On the Spiritual in Art, *concerning Cezanne's still-life painting. 'He made a living thing out of a teacup. To be more precise, he realized the existence of a being in this cup. He raised the* nature morte *to a height where the exteriorly "dead" object becomes inwardly alive.'*

palette knife to create the forms.

Between the Salon des Refusés and the first Impressionist exhibition in 1874, Cézanne became more closely associated with the Café Guerbois group and their friends. His closest associate was Pissarro but Manet was also becoming an influence. His attachment and participation in the development of Impressionism came as late as 1872–73 while he was staying at Pontoise with Pissarro. The painting which signalled that attachment was *The House of the Hanged Man* (plate 7), mentioned earlier, where the influence of Pissarro can clearly be seen, and their discussions on the Impressionist's use of paint led to the direct change in technique in this second stage in Cézanne's development. Through the 1870s, Cézanne's Impressionism changed into an analytical examination rather than visual perception, and when he abandoned the Parisian scene in 1877 to return to Aix, his isolation and intellectual concentration, undisturbed by the artistic conversation of the café life of Paris, enabled him to pursue the *petite sensation* of his *motif.*

To understand this mature stage in his art, it is necessary to go to Cézanne's own words for clues rather than specific information since, as we have noted earlier, words will not elucidate the nature of a painter's art. Perhaps the most significant observation he made, which bears not only upon his own philosophy but has been a foundation block in much of the modern structure of taste

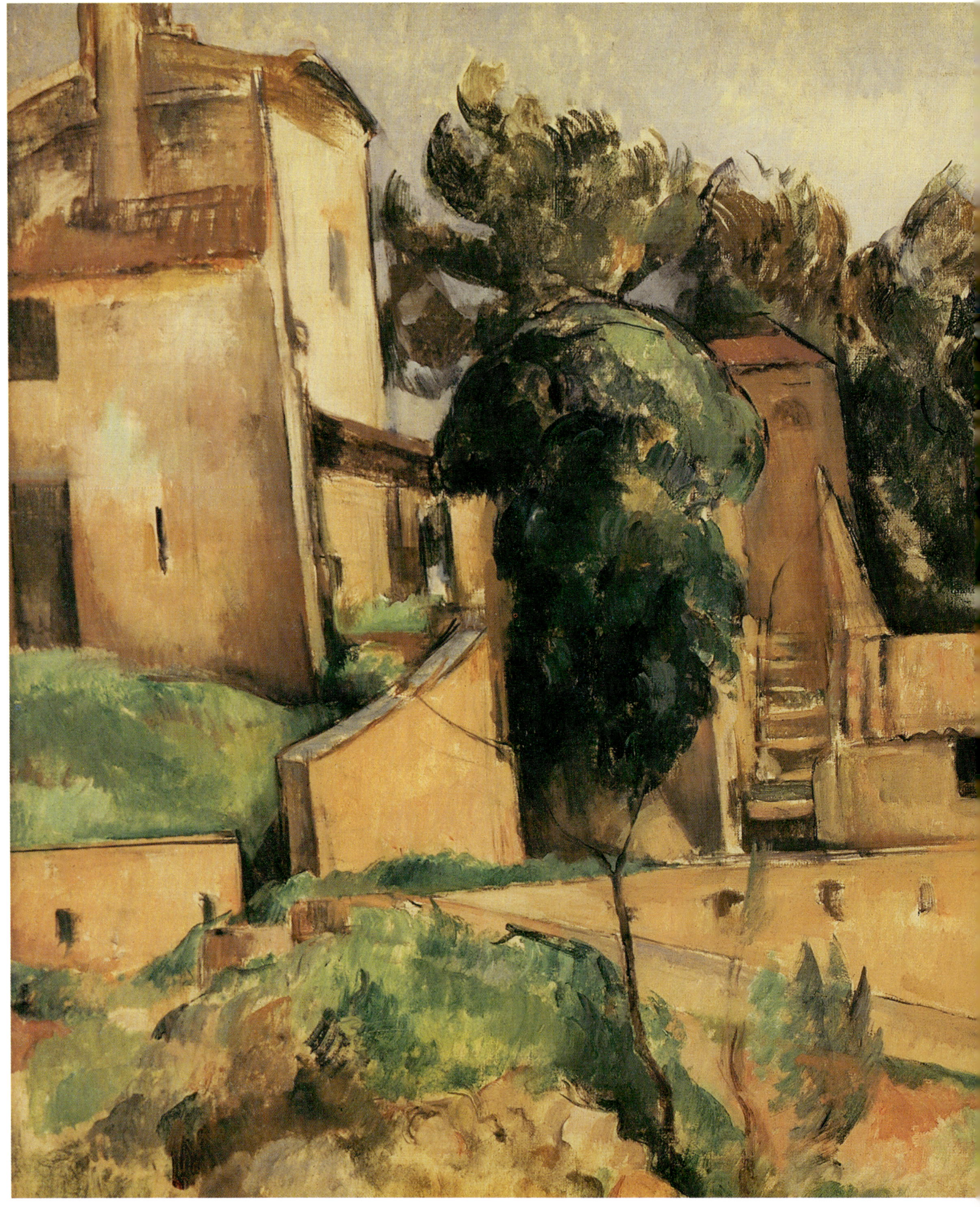

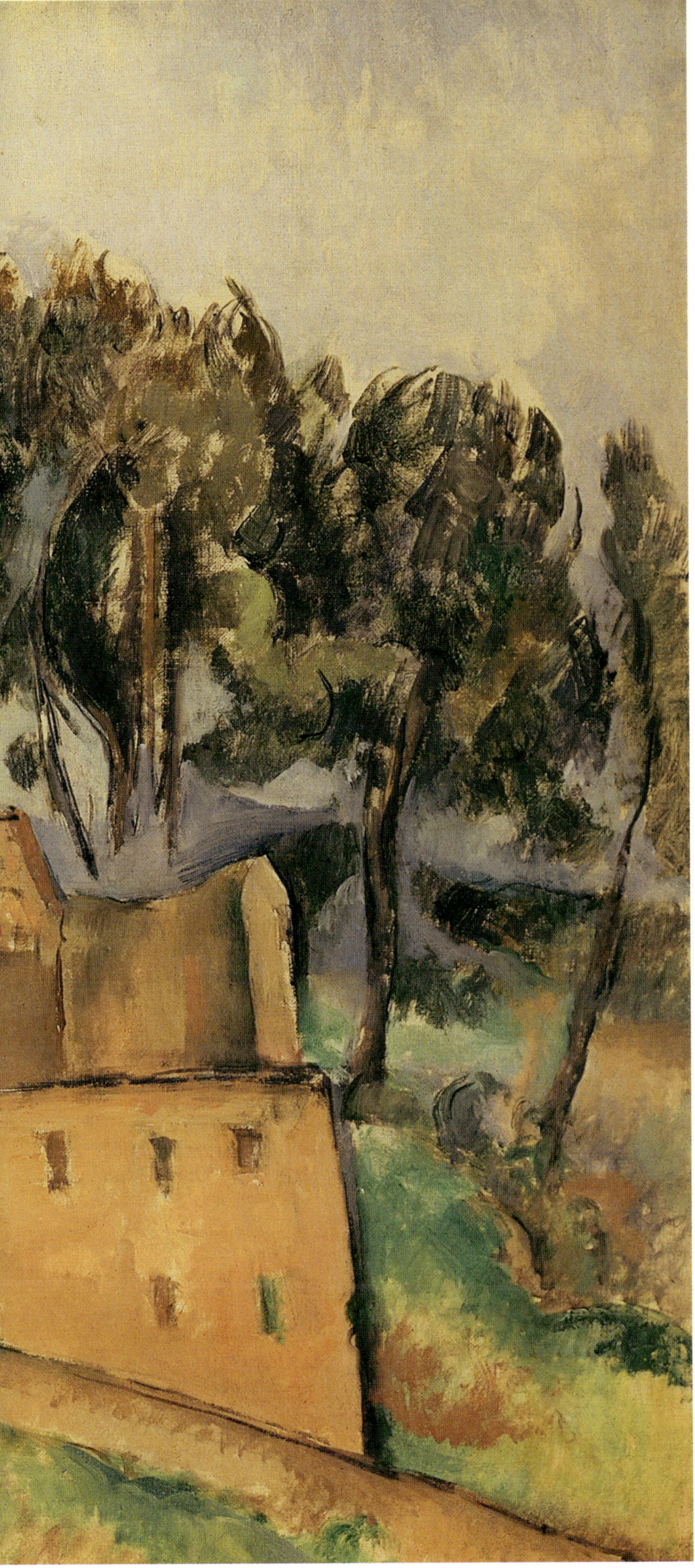

PLATE 30

The House of Bellevue (1890–92)

Oil on canvas, $25^{1}/_{2}$ x 32 inches (64.8 x 81.2cm)

Around 1885, Maxime Conil (married to Cézanne's sister Rose) bought an estate farm called Bellevue, south-west of Aix and situated on a hill dominating the whole of the wide valley of the river Arc and looking towards Mont Sainte-Victoire. As may be imagined, it was a favourite location for Cézanne to paint and it was from here that he painted a number of his views of the great mountain and the valley. He also painted several views of the farm, the house and the pigeonnier. *On the hill of Bellevue he could see a number of the* motifs *that engaged his interest over the years. The is one of two paintings made around the same time and reveal Cézanne's methods of construction. In the distant unfinished view, the firm lines of the picture structure are being established while the trees and shrubs surrounding the house are at an early stage of construction. The small linear strokes are suggesting further definition of the shrub forms without precluding a closer placing relating to the linear forms of the buildings. In this work, the house dominates from a close view and the relationships have been resolved in what is a complicated geometrical structure. But although the painting is well advanced there are, as usual, some small and larger areas of uncovered canvas. While Cézanne would not have considered it 'finished', in all probability he was not able to add further to the painting.*

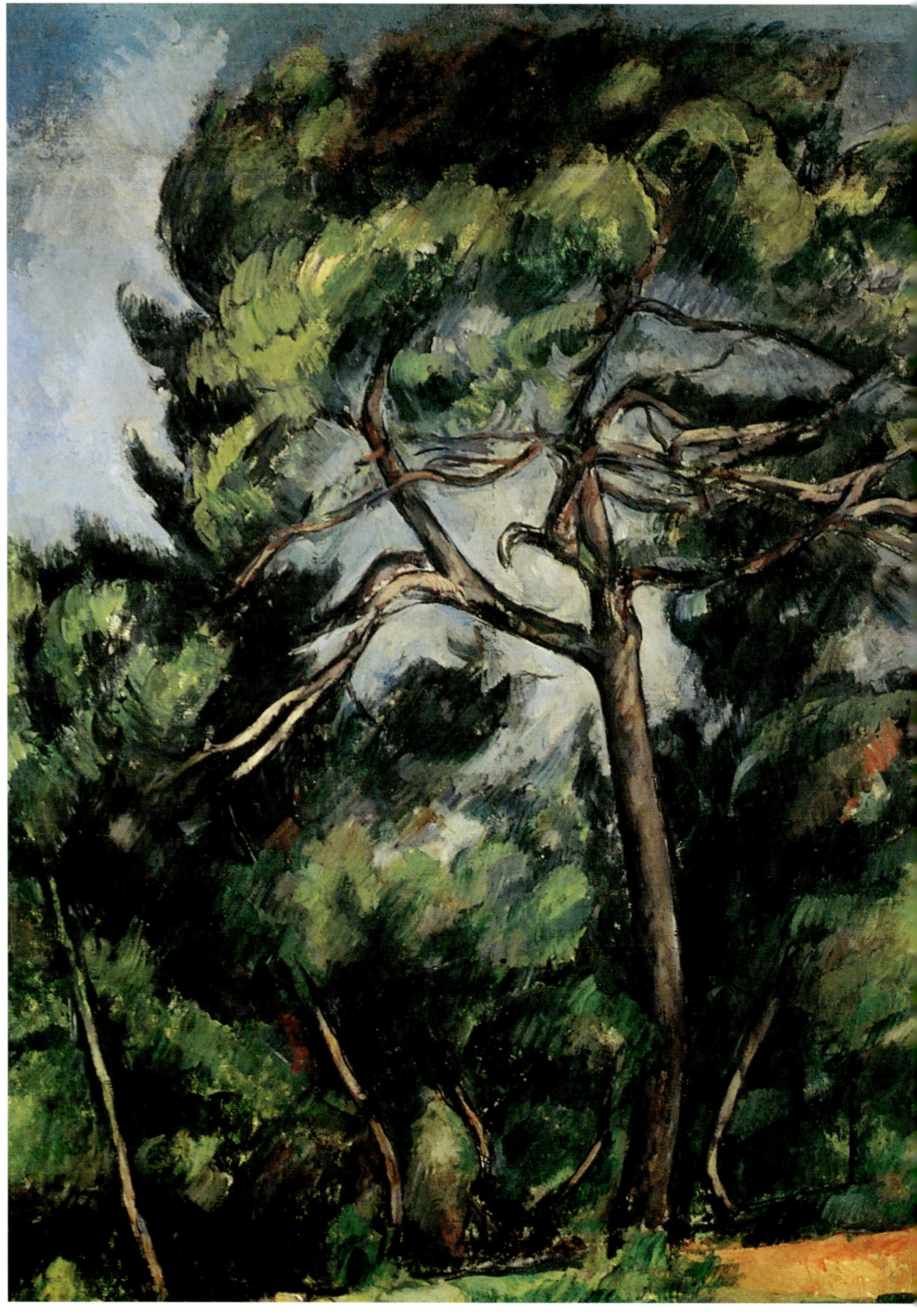

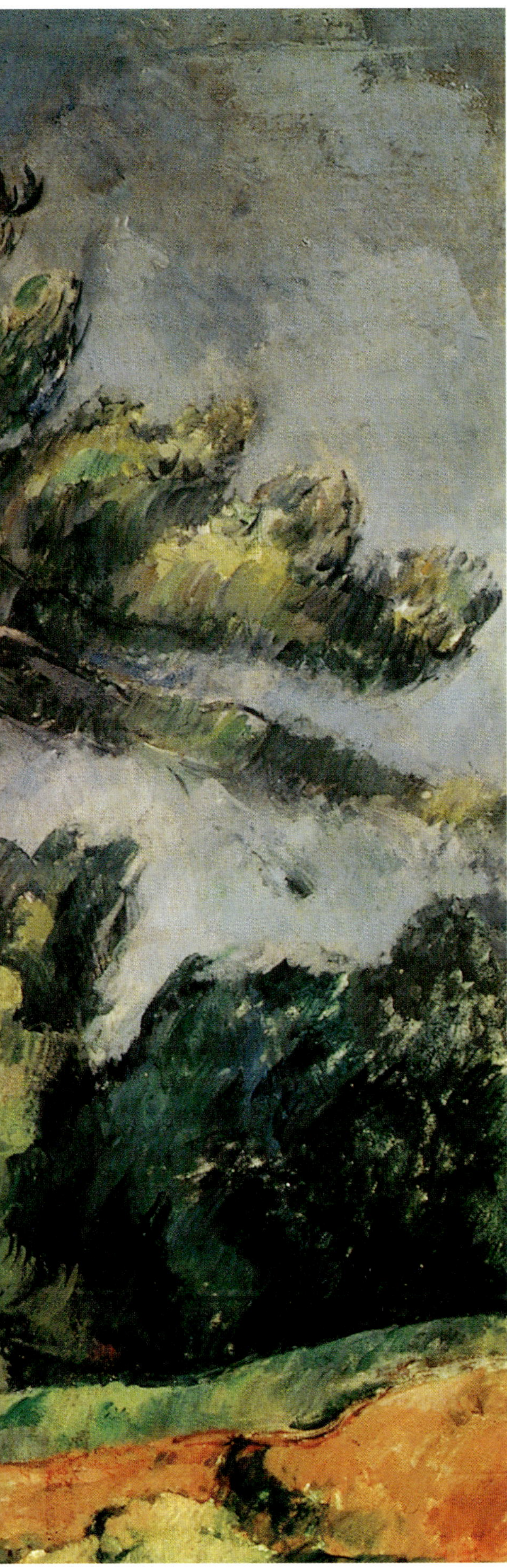

PLATE 31
The Great Pine (c.1889)
Oil on canvas, $33^1/_2$ x $36^1/_4$ inches (85 x 92cm)

Joachim Gasquet was the first owner of this painting and it reminded him of walks taken with Cézanne around Aix. As will be recalled, pine trees appeared regularly in Cézanne's paintings of the area. He made a number of drawings of single pines and a few paintings of which this work is a highly impressive example. The sense of pictorial identity, the implication of this fierce life-force in pictorial form is remarkable. It has been suggested that with this single study of a pine tree, formed as much by the elements as by its life-force, Cézanne may have been thinking of the painting by Monet of a similar tree subject. (Monet was the only living painter that Cézanne actively admired.) There is information on the development of this painting. Originally the painting only contained about two-thirds of the tree, the top being cut off by the top edge; but Cézanne then felt the need to open the painting to introduce more sky and successively added two bands of canvas, which may be discerned in the reproduction.

and art criticism was: 'Art is a harmony, parallel with the harmony of nature.' This suggests that he saw art, not as a casual observation of natural form – which would not place art in parallel to the harmony of nature – but to the superficial identification of varying surface experiences which of themselves were only the accident of locality. For Cézanne, the essential structure of the picture was to be drawn from the unity (harmony) of the whole of the experience of nature as drawn out of the selected *motif.* Such a search was pictorially unrelated directly to the creation of illusionist space, accidental effects of light, temporary colour and painting technique or pigment application. The painting for him became the object carrying the message, not the landscape that sponsored it. Far from light and atmosphere fracturing form, as had been the aim of the Impressionists, for Cézanne the elemental basic volumes were his own basis for the pictorial construction of his *motif.* It is not to be supposed that he looked for underlying geometric forms on which to construct his image, as has been construed from his letter to Bernard to 'treat nature by the cylinder, the sphere, the cone', but that these should be in mind as a guide to rendering his immediate perception, which is implied when he says 'sensations form the foundation of my work'. It is important to note that the forms he suggested should be used – the cylinder, sphere and cone – are curved in movement in space, not in conjoined or

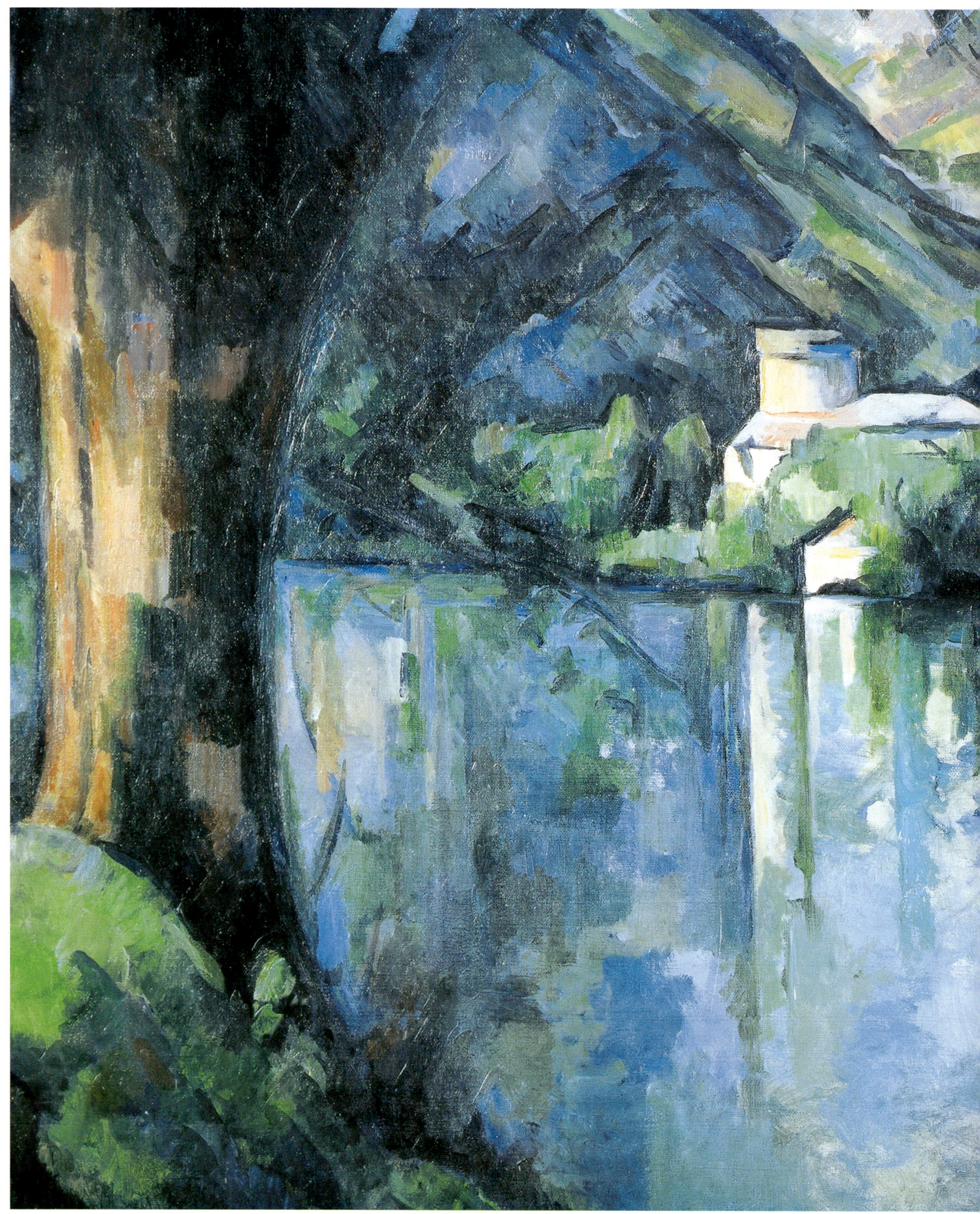

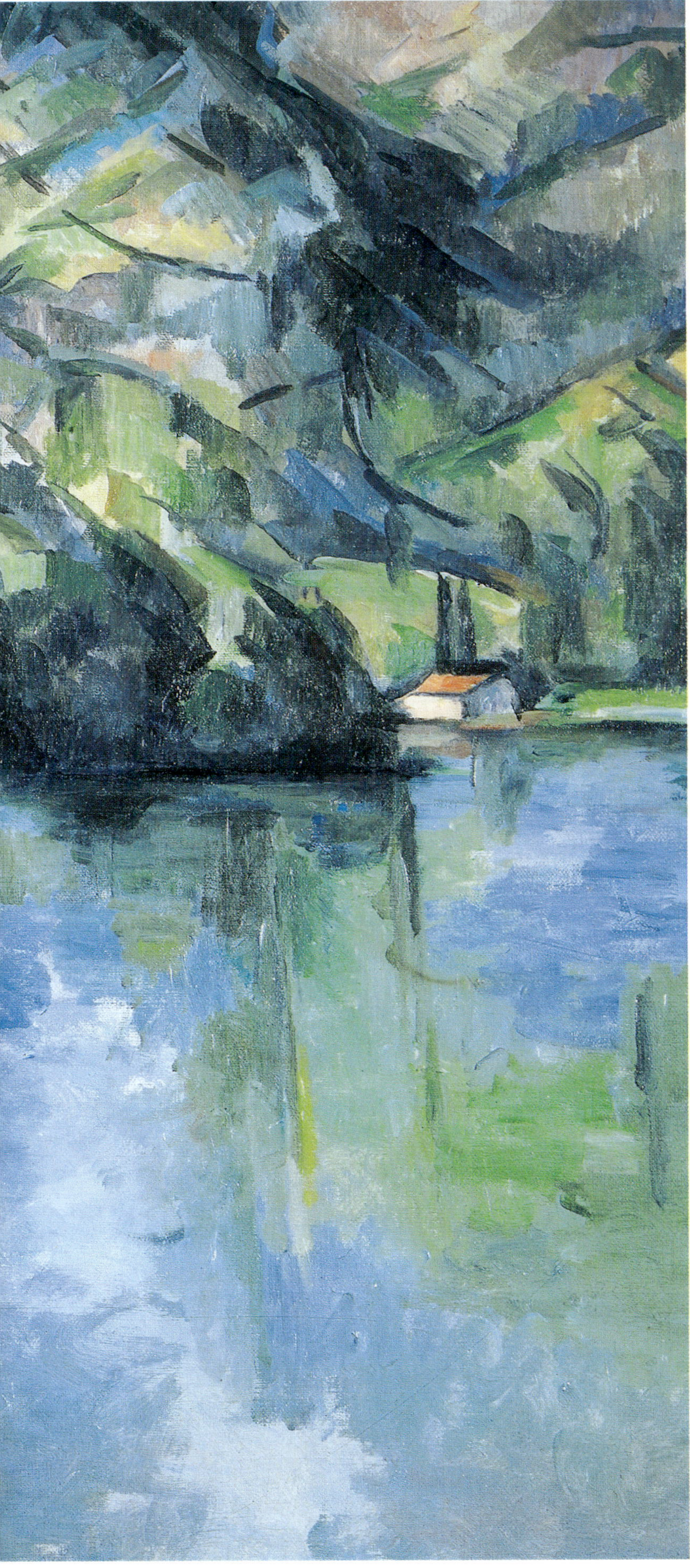

PLATE 32

The Lac d'Annecy (1896)

Oil on canvas, $25^{1}/_{4}$ x $31^{1}/_{8}$ inches (64.2 x 79.1cm)

Cézanne sold this painting to Ambroise Vollard soon after he had completed it. It shows the Château de Duingt on the side of the lake with the hills rearing behind it. It creates a feeling of claustrophobia without the release of any sky and the strong directional strokes make the circularity of the composition around the château hub evident, emphasized by the curved implication of the tree-trunk. The verticals in this painting descend from the horizontal (rather than rise from it as is more usual) and this is another indication of the psychological effect that linear direction and relationship held for Cézanne and made explicit in Seurat's theory that 'lines descending from the horizontal give sadness'. There is certainly an air of quiet nostalgia and remoteness in this exquisite work. Cézanne stayed at the small town of Talloires, in the Savoie, near the lake, and wrote to his friend Gasquet from there, noting the height of the mountains and the lake narrowed by two gorges. Others have remarked on the daunting mountains and the deep menace of the lake. This was the only painting Cézanne completed in Talloires.

PLATE 33

Still-Life with Fruit Basket (The Kitchen Table) (c.1888–89)

Oil on canvas, $25^{1}/_{2}$ x 32 inches (64.7 x 81.2cm)

This is an unusually complex, and in some ways unresolved work with a more than usual number of objects contained within it. Neither the perspective nor the physical positioning are consistent. As we have noted in other still-life paintings, the front table corners do not conjoin and there are other curiosities; the ellipses of the jars are at different eye-levels and the basket would not sit as placed on the table. The chair-leg on the right and the chair in the background do not sit in the created space. It is so different from other still-life works in its deep spatial exploration, rather than the usual flat wall which Cézanne places close behind his objects, that it seems to have been inspired by a different exploratory spirit. One could cite other instances of inconsistency or inaccuracy but nevertheless there remains an extraordinary authority and delight which convinces us of the pictorial rightness of the whole – what Cézanne called 'plastic equivalents' of reality.

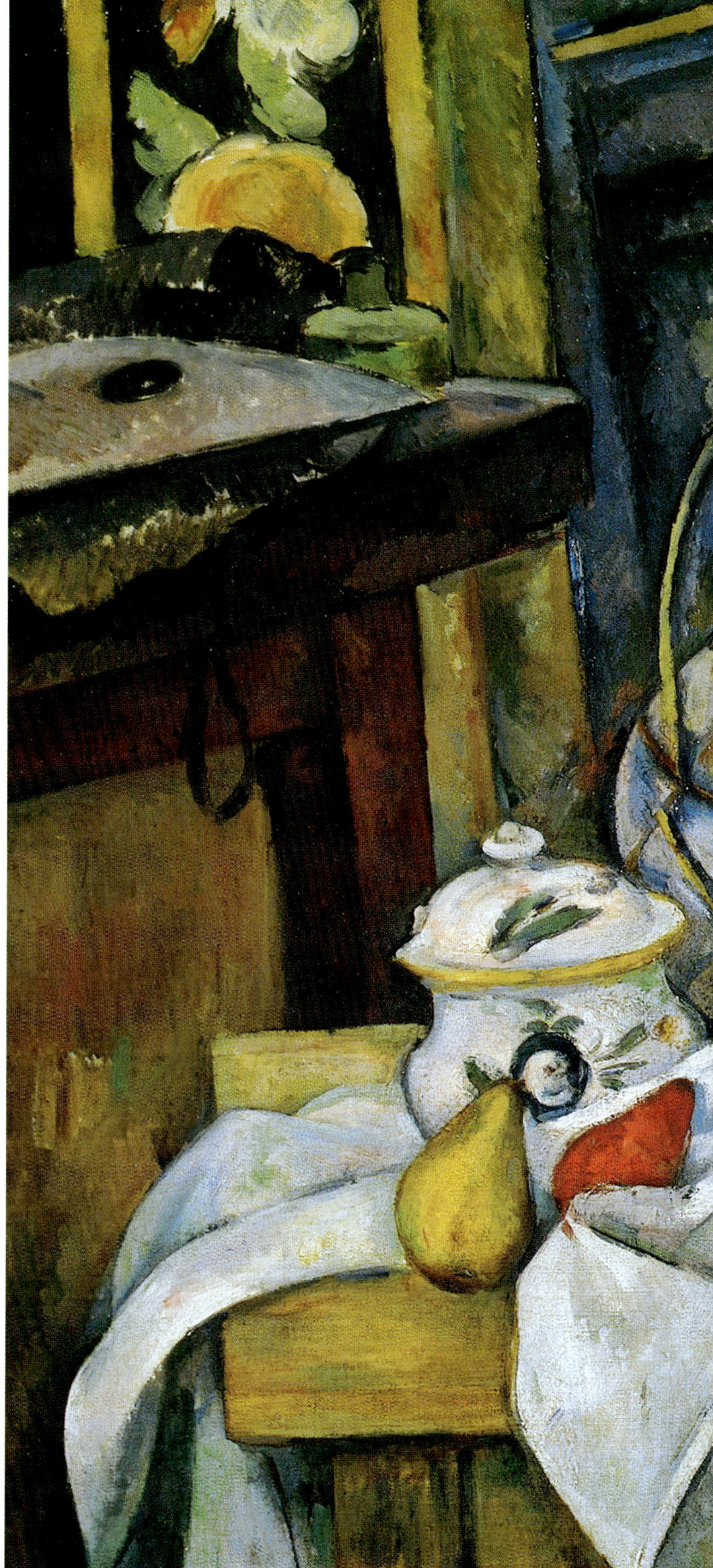

integrated flat planes. His injunction to 'treat' nature is thus one of sequential change – movement in space flatly identified for the purposes of art. 'Painting is not only to copy the object, it is to seize a harmony between numerous relations.' This was for him an objective with profound difficulties. So profound, that a single spot of colour could unbalance the carefully constructed harmony of the whole. As he confessed, 'I cannot attain the intensity that is unfolded before my eyes.' This explains why, when Vollard questioned him about two small spots of white canvas on his hands in the portrait, Cézanne explained that he could decide what they should be without further reference – and they still remain unpainted. (*See plate 41.*)

Cézanne said, 'I advance all my canvas at one time together.' This is so that at every stage it is as complete at that stage as it can be – one false building block and the edifice disintegrates or, as Cézanne puts it, 'There must not be a single link too loose, not a crevice through which may escape the emotion, the light, the truth.' From this emerges the essential element in Cézanne's painting. There is a truth which is the painting, not the subject, not the object but the single identity of the painting which is complete as itself – or as complete as it exists undefiled at any stage in its growth.

It should be said that it is this 'flat space' – the

Continued on page 65

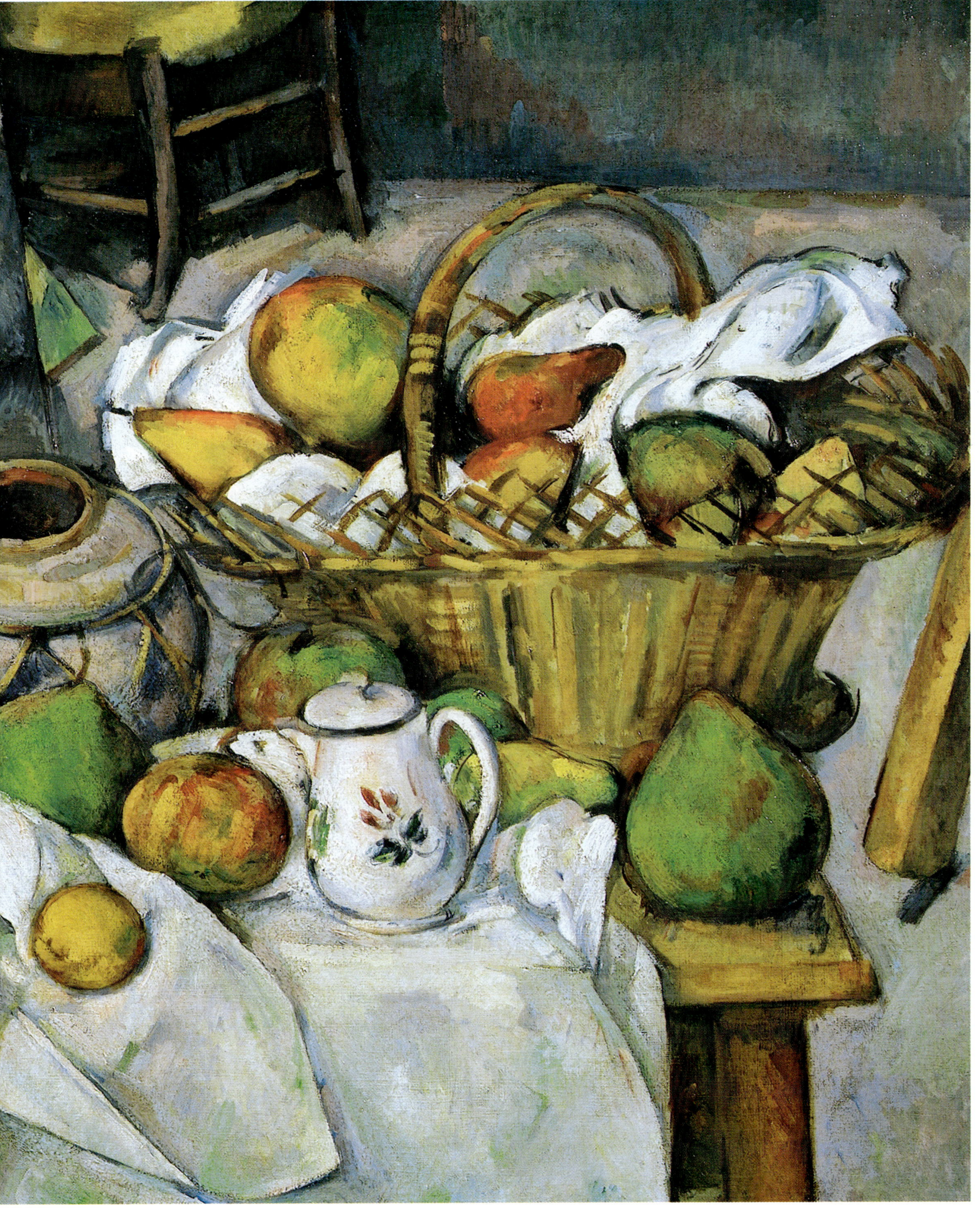

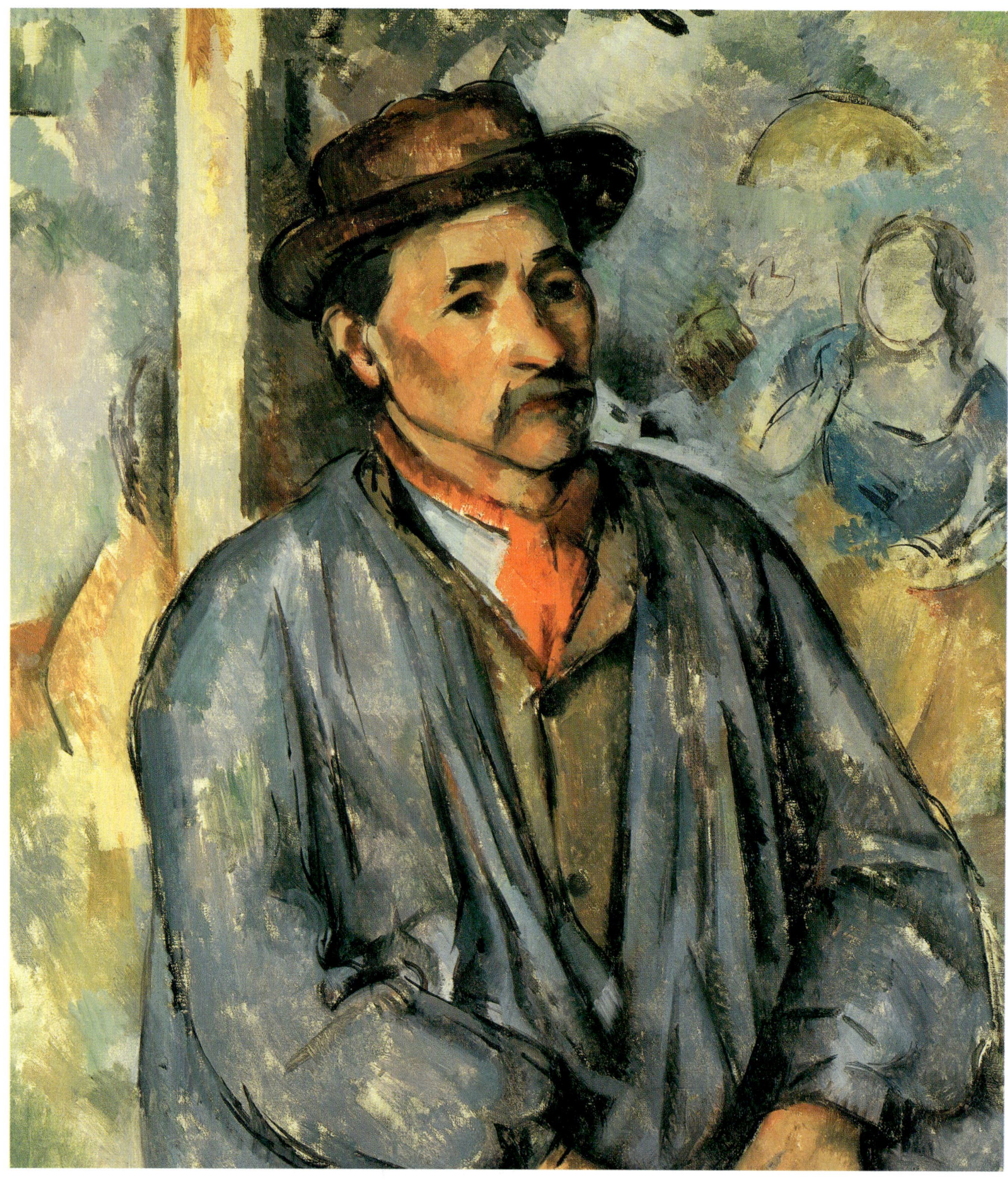

PLATE 34

Peasant in a Blue Smock (c. 1895–1900)

Oil on canvas, $31\frac{7}{8}$ x $25\frac{1}{2}$ inches (81 x 65cm)

During the later 1880s and 1890s Cézanne often used local people as models as his interest in portraiture and his devotion to his local landscape continued to engross him. Peasant in a Blue Smock *is part of the Mont Sainte-Victoire landscape. This individual appears in two of the Card Players paintings and was evidently someone who in his passive stolidity interested Cézanne. He is seated here in front of what seems to be an unexpectedly elegant female carrying a parasol. In fact, it is a detail of a screen that Cézanne had painted for Jas de Bouffan many years earlier when his father first purchased the house. Some of the portraits were painted in Jas de Bouffan and it seems that Cézanne was intrigued by the relationship of the phlegmatic sitter to the unfamiliar sophistication that surrounded him. Cézanne's practice of not continuing horizontal edges, as can be noted in plate 20, is present in this painting in a different form. The left-hand edge of the smock below the arm, and its width inside the arm, do not coincide with the physical structure of the sitter; but the whole corresponds to the pictorial unity of the peasant's image. An indication that Cézanne's work was appreciated by his friends is apparent in an observation that Gasquet made when he saw the painting in Cézanne's studio: 'One especially, in a blue smock, decked out in a red foulard, his arms dangling, is admirable in his ruggedness, like the materialized thought of a bit of earth that's suddenly been incarnated in this crude and magnificent flesh, cooked by the sun and whipped by the wind.'*

PLATE 35

Portrait of Madame Cézanne

(c.1885–90) detail

Oil on canvas, $31\frac{7}{8}$ x $25\frac{1}{2}$ inches (81 x 65cm)

Cézanne painted his wife a number of times during their long relationship, both before and after their marriage in 1886. In these rather simple, thinly painted works, the character of a study is more evident than of a fully resolved work. This was executed when Hortense was in her late 30s and they reveal a mature woman with a peaceful nature.

It was in 1886 that Zola published his novel in which his central figure is the artist Claude Lantier, based on Cézanne. In the book, the model and wife of Lantier is Christine Hallegrin and it seems that Zola had Hortense in mind when he created the character. He describes her thus: '...a tall supple and slim girl, still a little thin in body... A brunette with black hair and black eyes. The upper part of the face very gentle, with great tenderness. Long eye-lids, pure and tender forehead, small and delicate nose... But the lower part of her face is passionate, the jaw a little prominent, too strong ...'

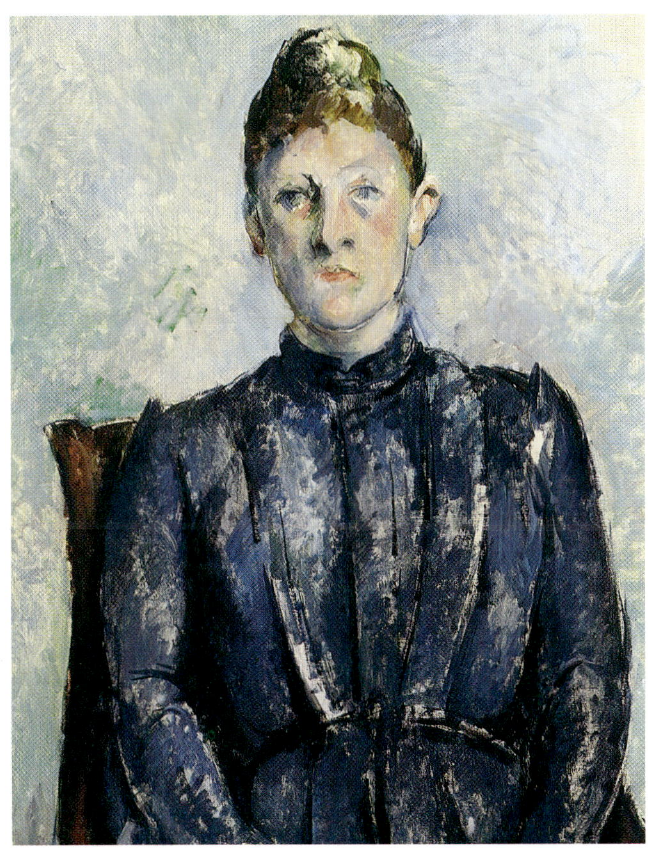

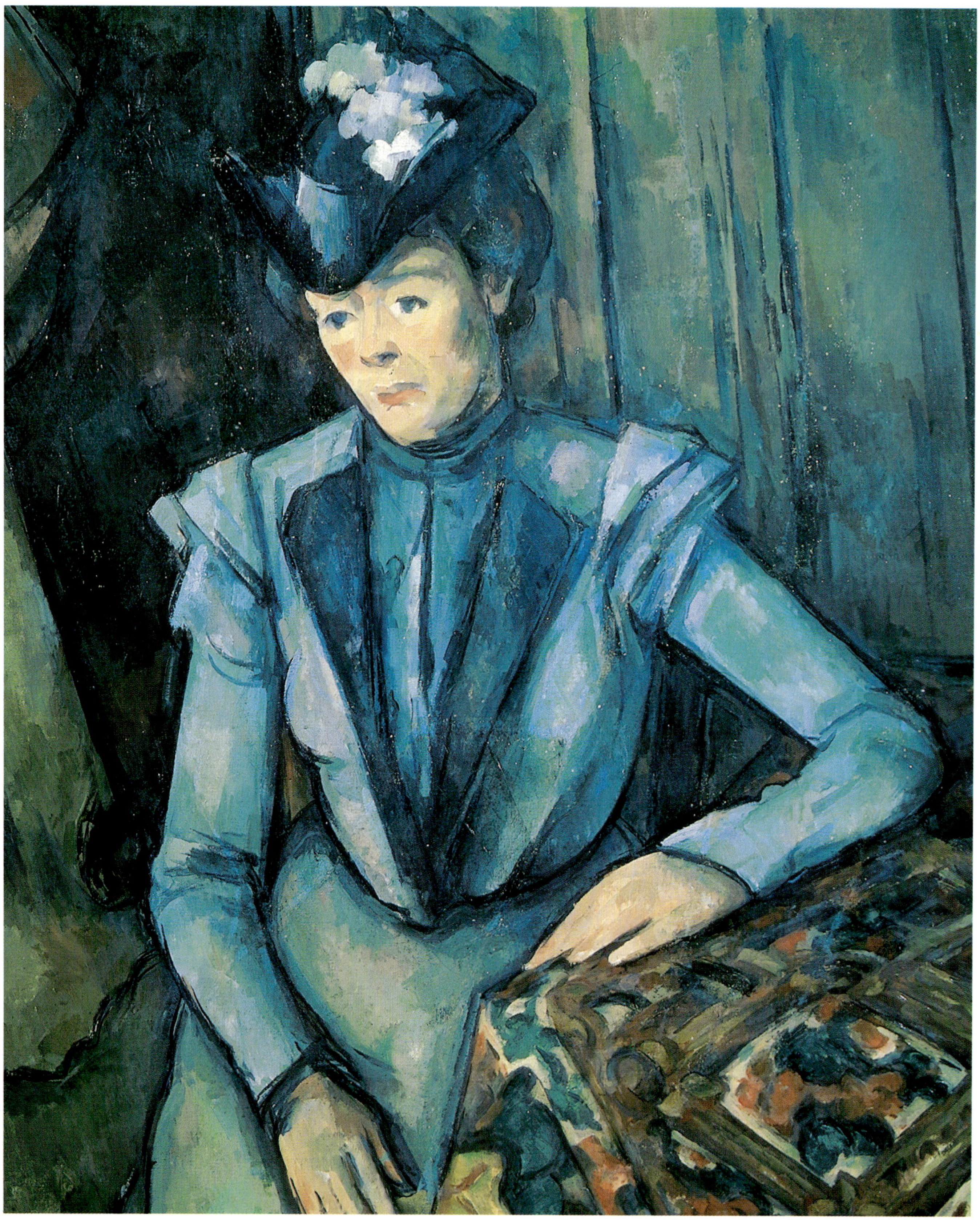

PLATE 36

Woman in Blue (before 1899, or 1900–04)

Oil on canvas, $34^{5}/_{8}$ x $28^{1}/_{3}$ inches (88.5 x 72cm)

There is considerable uncertainty surrounding this painting. It was dated around 1895 but recently has been redated to soon after 1900 and was painted either in Cézanne's rented studio in the rue Boulegon or in his new studio in Chemin des Lauves. It has been suggested that it is a portrait of Hortense – the usual assumption when the sitter is unknown – but this is now discounted; the figure is too stylish and the volume of the head and its features resemble none of the portraits of his wife. The structure of the painting is very tightly organized and fully painted and is unusual in at least one respect; the face is depicted with a clear expression and there is an apparent search for a likeness rather than the overall structural identity so common in Cézanne's portraits. Analysis of the background is more than difficult: the forms are unidentifiable, the dark area mysterious, and the purpose of the wavy line (seemingly unrelated) is obscure. There is one feature encountered elsewhere; the table-top edge appears to be at two angles, a distortion that Cézanne frequently arrives at for the clear identification of relationships. In this painting one can discern the seeds of Cubism.

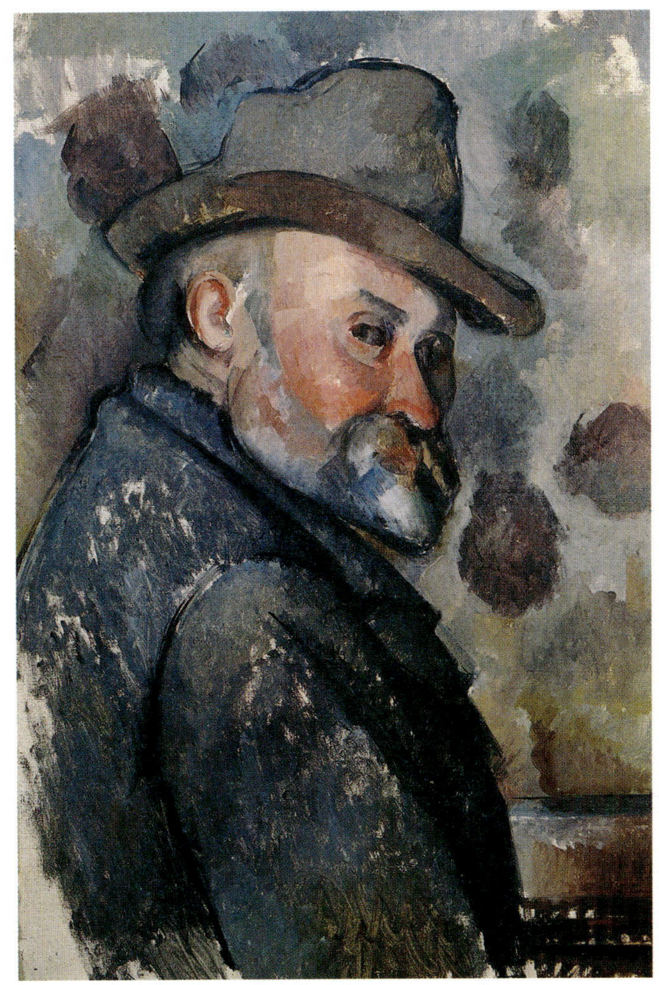

PLATE 37

Self-Portrait in Felt Hat (1890–94)

Oil on canvas, $23^{2}/_{3}$ x $19^{1}/_{4}$ inches (60 x 49cm)

As in Peasant in a Blue Smock *(plate 34), there are small areas in this painting that are uncovered and here it is clearly not for any other reason than that Cézanne could not decide what to place there in each location. He has worked steadily on the head which is, apart from an area near the ear, completely realized. The coat is, however, unresolved; the shape of the arm is integrated but its identity is not and, since he could not resolve it, he stopped. Or if this is not so, and there is no evidence on the point, there is certainly some reason since it would have taken any other painter of the time a minute or so to have taken the uncovered areas to a finished stage. There is a different pictorial dynamic in this self-portrait from that in the previous works illustrated (plates 11 and 13). There is a sliding temporary character here, a spiky sense of movement which contrasts with the other versions. The subject is the same, recognizably, but the painting is different in pictorial not representational content. It is an explanation of Cézanne's importance.*

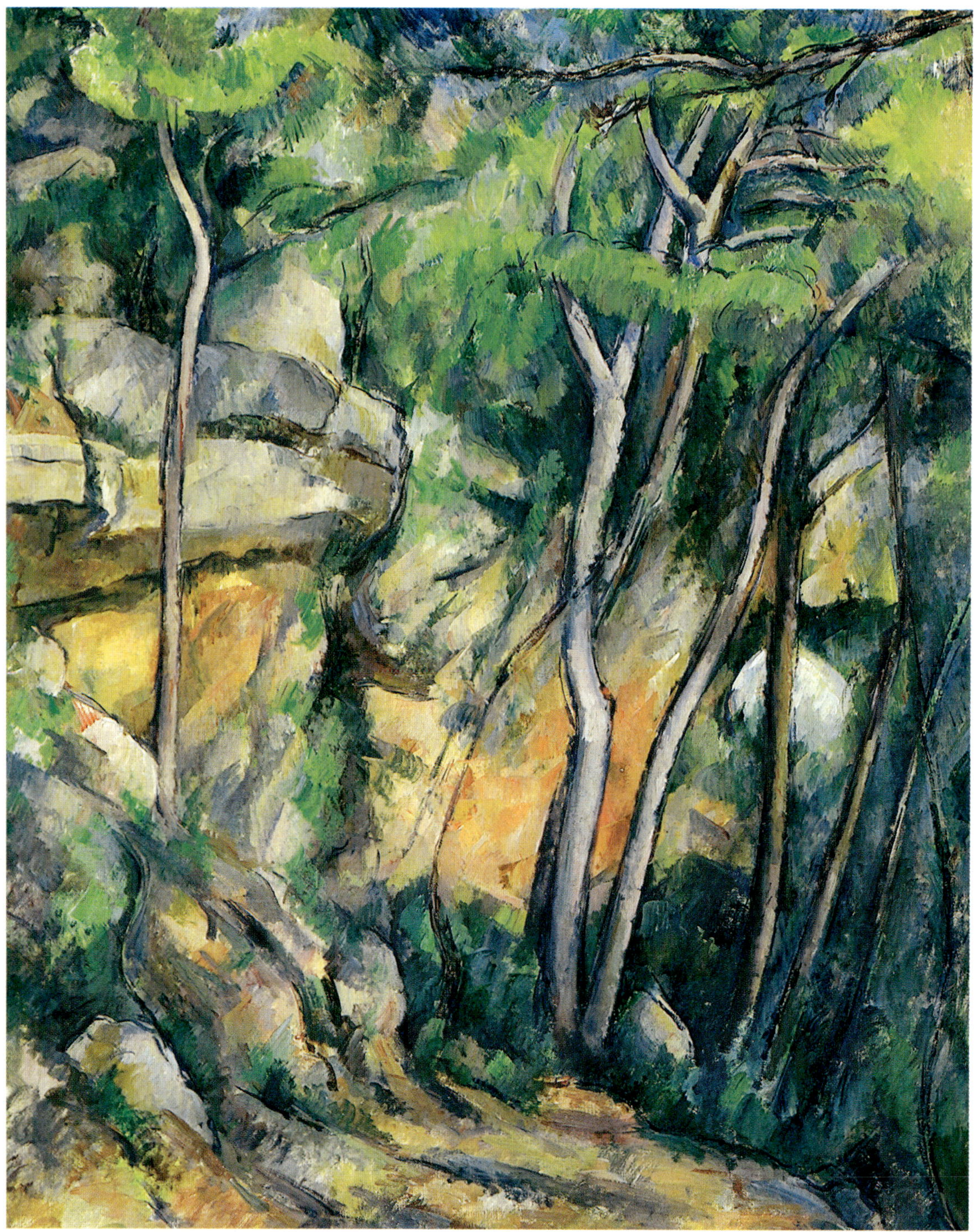

PLATE 38

In the Grounds of the Château Noir

(c.1899) detail

Oil on canvas, $36^{1}/_{4}$ x $28^{3}/_{4}$ inches (92 x 73cm)

When their mother died in 1897, his sister Marie took charge of settling Cézanne's affairs and under pressure from her brother-in-law Maxime Conil agreed to the sale of Jas de Bouffan. This changed the pattern of Cézanne's life, depriving him of his one settled home and the centre of his painting life. Henceforward, from 1899 until almost the end of his life, he lived unhappily, something of a displaced person in a number of different rented accommodations. The Château Noir, halfway between Aix and Le Tholonet was where he rented a small room from which he went on painting expeditions looking for a motif *within its rocky wooded grounds. In order to find a permanent location he offered to buy the château but was refused. The painting illustrated is a fine example of Cézanne's landscape style at this period in his life. The closely-knit organization of the picture area, the keen search for internal relationships and the extraordinary sense of individual identity, all characteristics of his work, are apparent here. Note the surging strength of the sapling on the left against the solid blocks of rock, each supporting the living identity of the other.*

PLATE 39

The Bibémus Quarry (1898–1900)

Oil on canvas, $25^1/_2$ x $21^1/_4$ inches (65 x 54cm)

Another place that Cézanne rented after the sale of Jas de Bouffan was a small cabin in the Bibémus quarry which he had rented a few years earlier while in search of his motifs. *It is clear that in this painting his interest lay in the relationship between the bulbous tree shape, seeming almost like a gigantic flower, and the rock immediately below it, carrying the vertical continuation of the tree-trunk. The sense of relationship between the growing form and the immutable rock is palpable and carries echoes throughout the composition.*

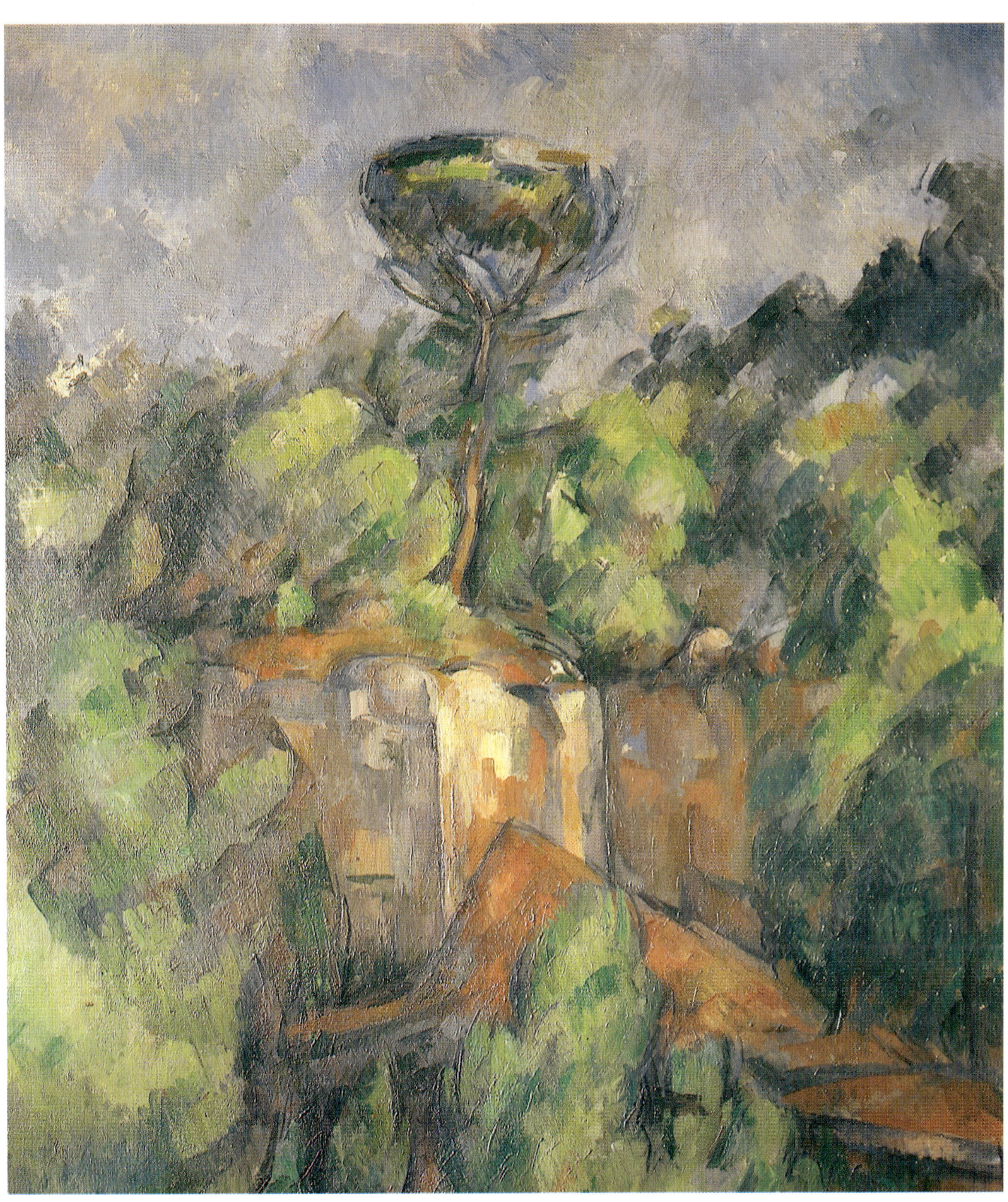

PLATE 40

Still-Life with Apples and Oranges (c. 1899)

Oil on canvas, 29 x 36$^{2}/_{3}$ inches (74 x 93cm)

Cézanne's later still-life paintings become increasingly elaborate and sumptuous and of them all this is perhaps the most richly conceived and painted with the greatest fluidity and assurance. All the features of Cézanne's treatment of this subject-matter are present. There is also an almost baroque feeling in the free disposition of the cloth and fruit which all seem almost to float in a frozen, flat space, emphasized by the high close angle from which it is viewed. The changes in the angle of perspective from front to back draws the viewer from the bottom towards the top (this is also encountered in Degas' late bather paintings) and into the picture space where the blank wall and decorative fabrics halt the eye. The patterned textile, a carpet, perhaps, is the same as the table covering in plate 36.

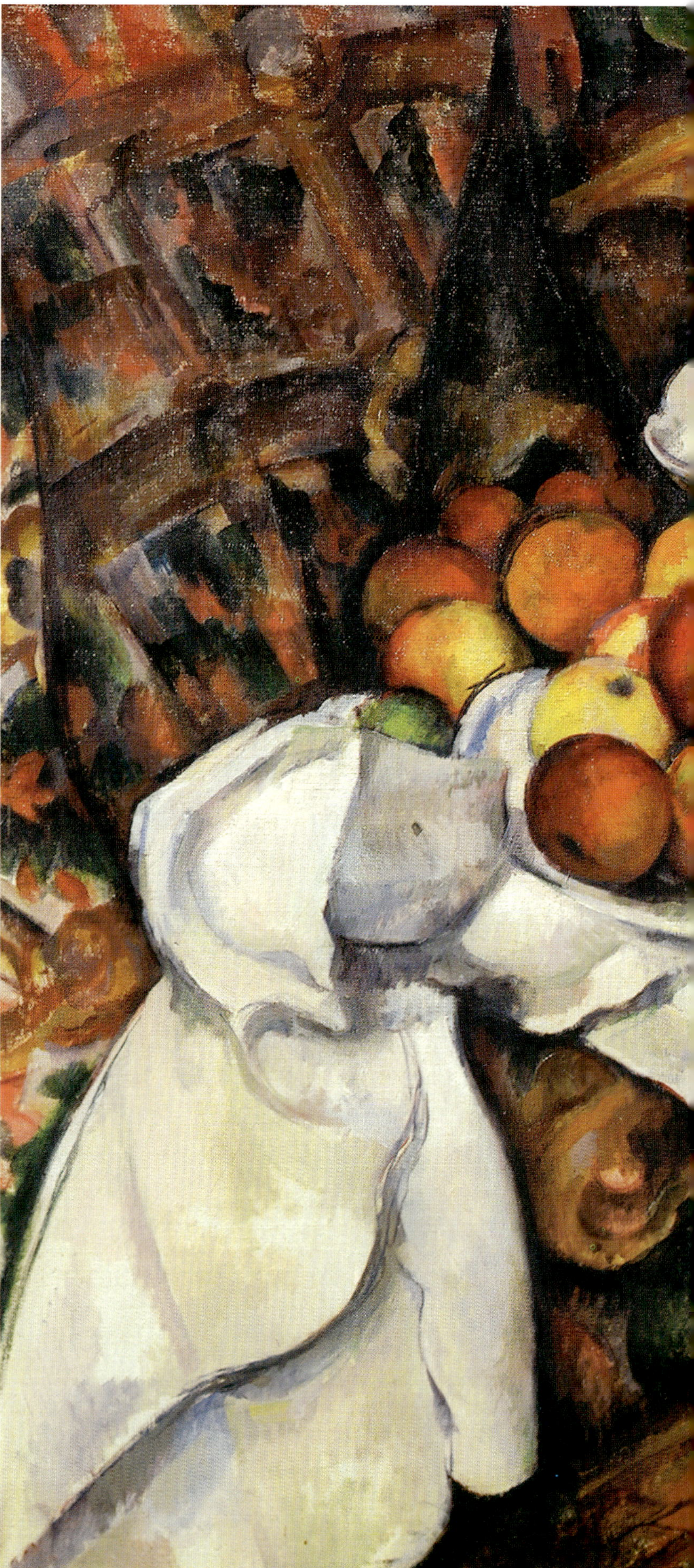

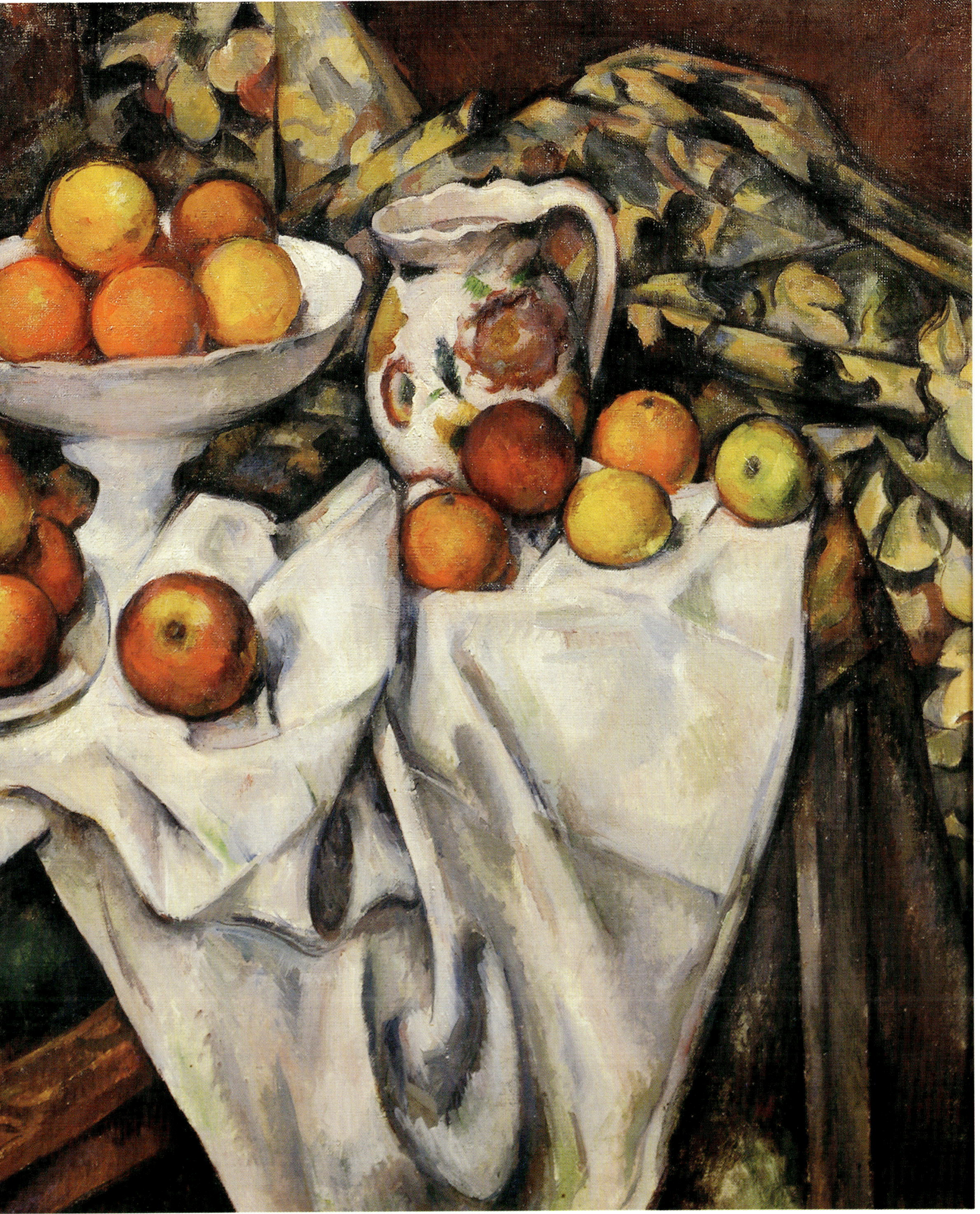

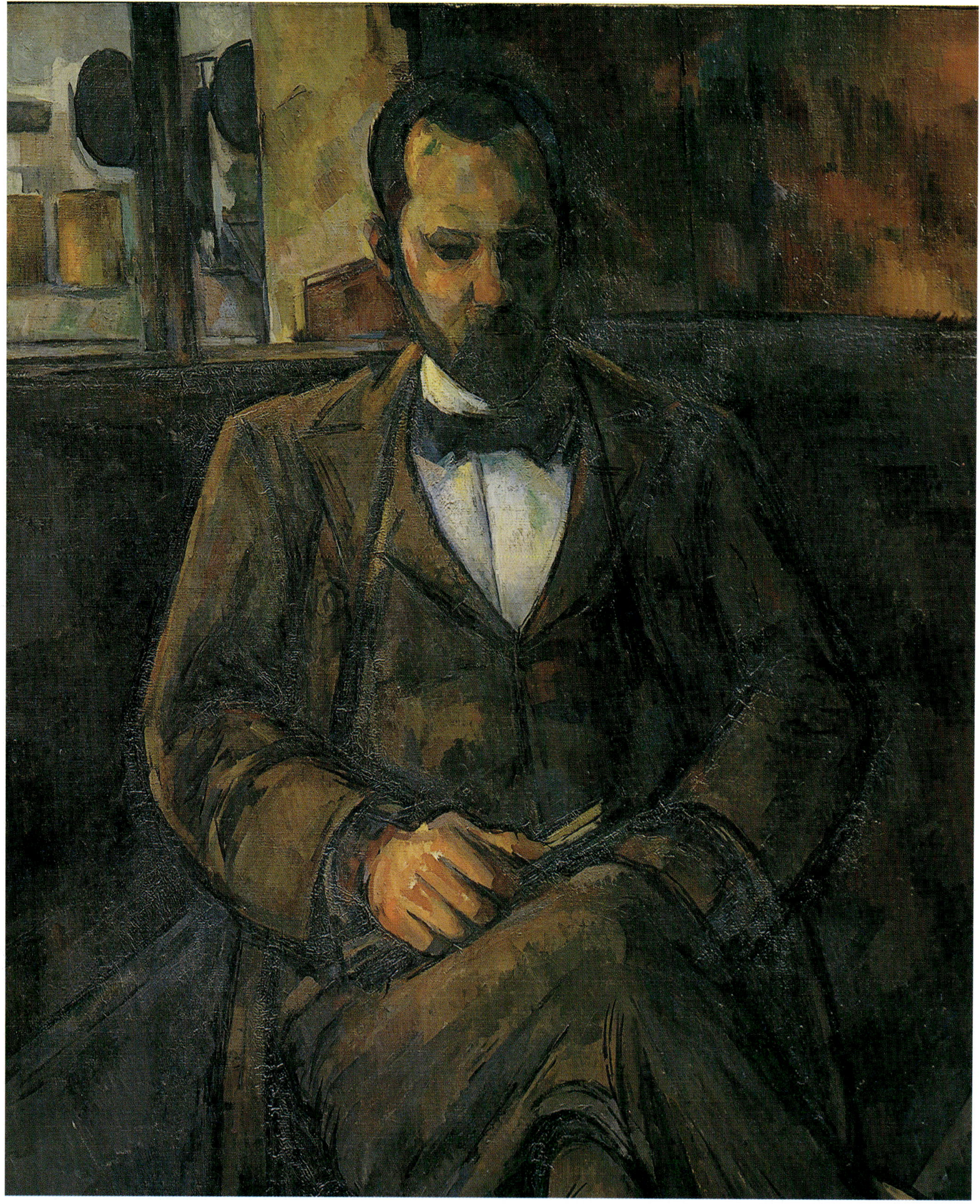

PLATE 41

Portrait of Ambroise Vollard (1899)

Oil on canvas, $39^{1}/_{2}$ x 32 inches (100.3 x 81.3cm)

Vollard made a number of comments in relation to this portrait in addition to the one mentioned in the introduction and they are all highly revealing of Cezanne's procedures. Cézanne's reply to another observation which Vollard made on the patches of bare canvas showing through the hands is also revealing: '...if I put something there by guesswork I might have to paint the whole canvas over again, starting from that point.' The bare patches are still there, Vollard made no further observations, and kept so quiet that he drifted into sleep and shifted his body which prompted the famous rebuke, 'Wretch! You're changing the pose! I say to you in all truth, you must remain still like an apple. Does an apple fidget?' The composition is based on a cruciform, popular with Cézanne, the horizontal of which, on a slightly different level on either side of the head, is balanced by a clear off-vertical running from above the head through the division in the famous shirt-front, the jacket and finishing in the lower leg on the edge of the canvas. The pictorial structure suggests the first stages of the surface organization of a later Cubist composition by Picasso or Braque. The relationship between the shape of the shirt-front and Vollard's head emphasizes the significance that the shirt-front held for Cézanne in the tightly-knit composition.

Continued from page 54

individual picture identity – which has had such an important effect upon the most important of the modern pictorial developments. Put in a slightly more prosaic form, Maurice Denis' now famous dictum is appropriate here: 'Remember that a painting, before it is a horse, a nude or some sort of anecdote, is essentially a flat surface covered with colours arranged in a certain order.' For Cézanne, the consciousness of the identity of the art object (the canvas and paint) as distinct and separate was omnipresent as in itself the only pictorial reality. The finding of that unique separate identity was the core of Cézanne's struggle. This is revealed in many of his comments and observations as reported by his friends, notably Ambroise Vollard, who was also his dealer. One of the most entertaining and illuminating is Vollard's description of the painting process when Cézanne undertook his portrait. One story from the account is well known and revealing. After 115 sittings, in which Vollard was commanded to sit still like an apple: 'Apples don't move do they?' said Vollard, exhausted, but hopefully enquiring how the work was progressing. Cézanne replied, 'The front of the shirt is not bad.' That is worth thinking about. Incidentally, the portrait was never finished, the two white spots are still on the hand.

Émile Bernard, who late in Cézanne's life had many conversations with him and recorded much of what he said, described how Cézanne was in the habit of describing with his hands the meaning he intended – for instance as follows; 'I have my *motif* [he joins his hands]. A *motif*, you see, is this [he draws his hands apart, fingers spread out, and brings them together again, slowly; then joins them, presses them together and contracts them, making them interlace]. There you have it; that is what one must attain.'

For the last 30 years of his life, that pictorial presence to enfold his *motif* was worked through in some of the most influential works in the history of Western art. His subjects were not obscure or suggestive (at least for him) of some grander intellectual message; they existed in total justification as themselves.

Cézanne's remoteness from the recognized centre of art in Paris resulted in his achievements remaining unacknowledged until the next generation, as the new century approached, began to see in this hermit-like figure, qualities that were missing from the whole repertoire of Impressionist or academic painting. From the beginning of the century, the rise in Cézanne's reputation and influence began to increase and continues.

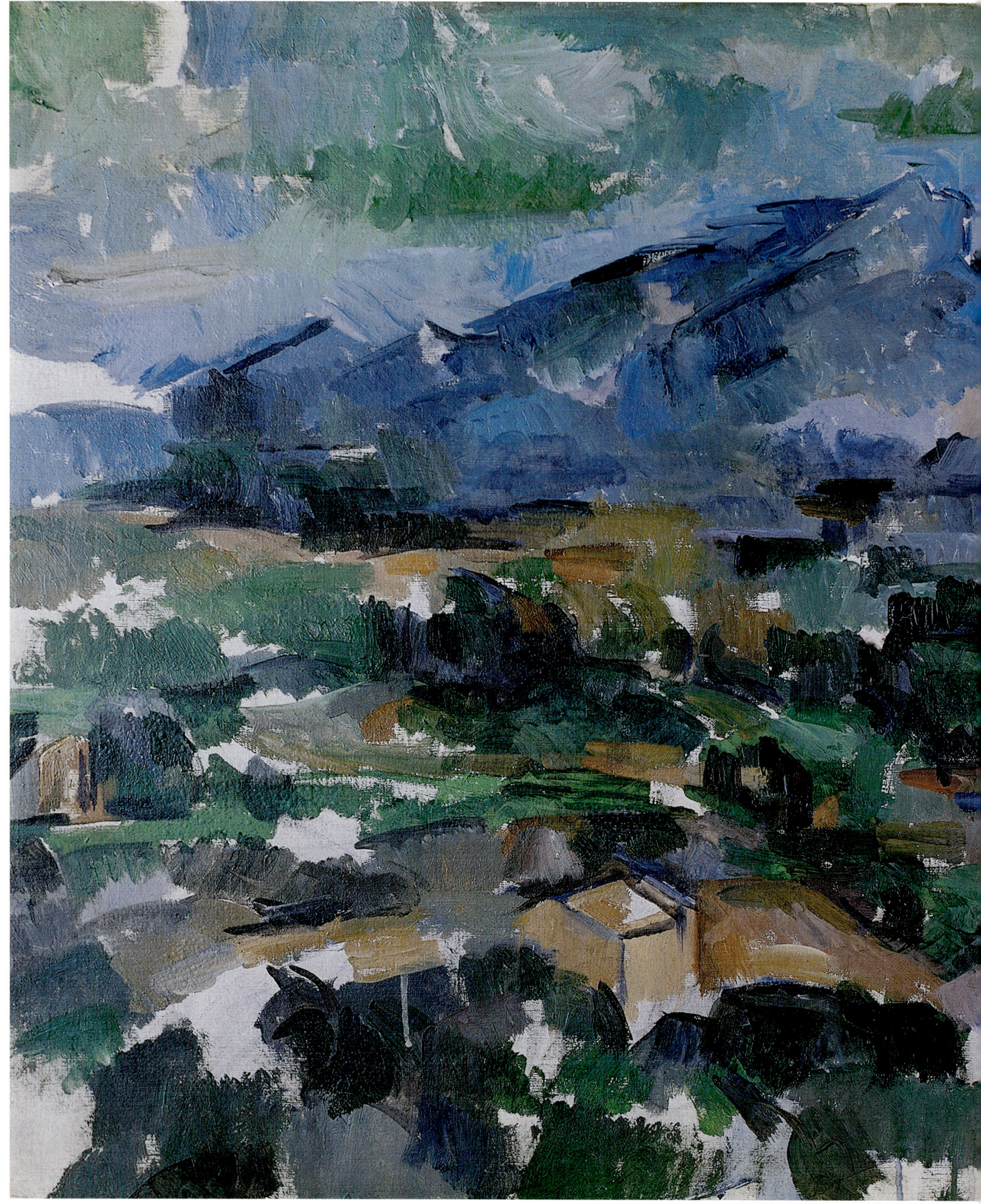

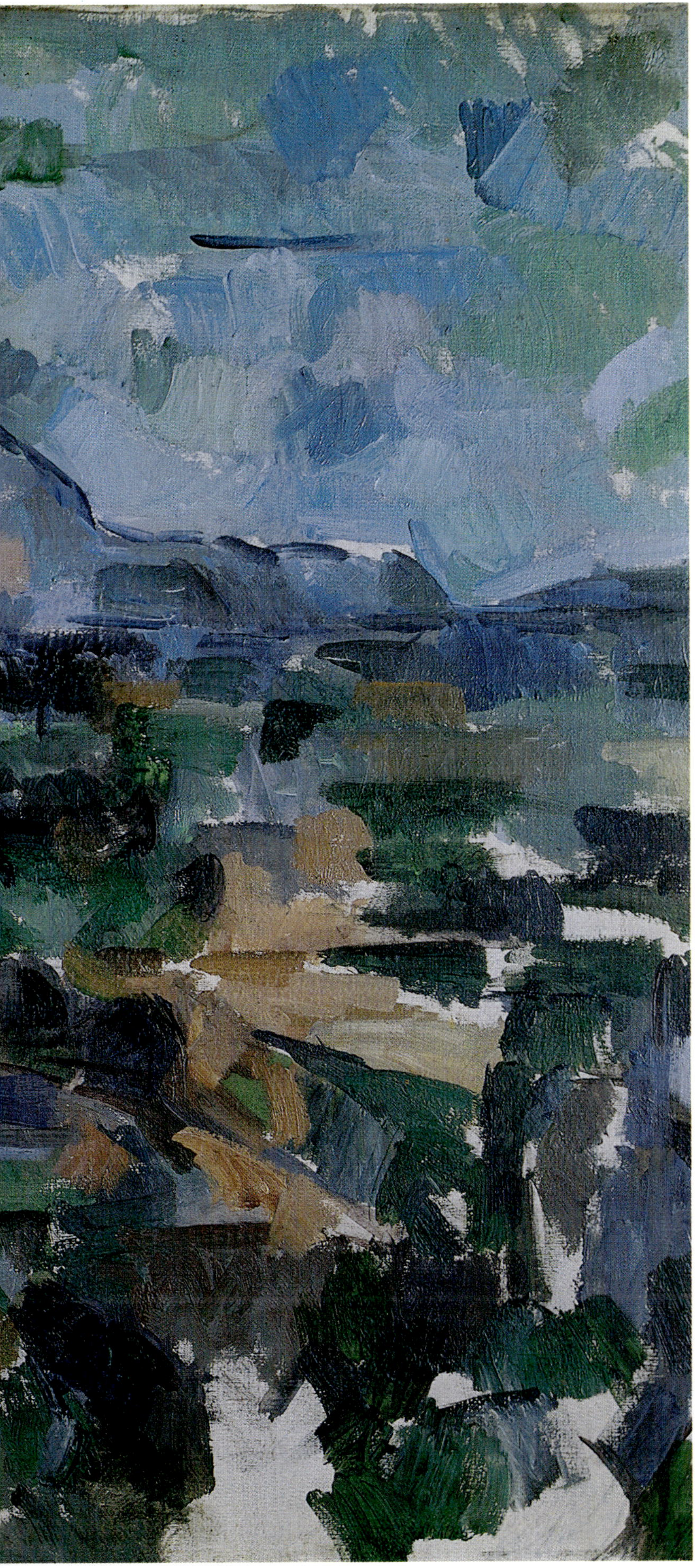

PLATE 42

Mont Sainte-Victoire (1904–05)

Oil on canvas, $23^{2}/_{3}$ x $28^{3}/_{4}$ inches (60 x 73cm)

In November 1901, Cézanne bought some land north of Aix-en-Provence with an extensive view of the town and the surrounding countryside including, of course, Mont Sainte-Victoire. On this site on the Chemin des Lauves he built a house with a large studio and high windows, opening south onto the town with another even larger window looking north. From 1902 Cézanne worked almost full-time in the studio from which he could see the mountain and where he began a last series of paintings in oil and watercolour of this early subject. It is, of course, interesting to compare the two series from slightly different viewpoints (see also plates 21, 43 and 44). Undoubtedly the Les Lauves view is the more dramatic; it rises on a gradual slope on the north and ends in an enormous rocky peak which falls away almost vertically towards the valley plain north-east of Aix where it is peopled by farms and fields interspersed with trees and copses. The scene seemed to have held for him the oppositions which defined his emotional and physical conflicts and he succeeds (in these paintings and drawings before his most significant subject) in achieving a resolution which provides the culmination of his pictorial odyssey. The struggle reduces itself into his synthesizing of nature into art and art as nature.

In the earlier series of the 1880s, Cézanne discovers and combines the various elements of the scene in which the mountain figures in relationship with the foreground pine trees and the middle-distant valley of the Arc with the viaduct, so that it dominates, but distantly, the pastoral scene. The structured space coincides with the pictorial identity, providing the unity and harmony that at that time was his intention and struggle.

In the later series of 11 paintings and a large number of watercolour and drawn sketches, a new priority has emerged. The art, that is the canvas and its paint, is the landscape, the motif, *that draws only what it needs from nature to enable it to live its own independent life. Maurice Denis, a friend who was with Cézanne in Aix for part of the time during the second series, made a watercolour study of Cézanne painting on the Les Lauves site. He was a painter and member of the Nabis group and he made a now well known observation that 'before a painting is a horse, a nude or some sort of anecdote it is essentially colours arranged on a flat surface in a certain order'. Cézanne's achievement is that he established the primacy of that order as the pictorial imperative. Much of 20th-century art depends from that achievement and, incidentally, explains the proposition offered at the beginning of the introduction to this book.*

PLATE 43

Mont Sainte-Victoire from Les Lauves

(1904–05)

Oil on canvas, $23^{2}/_{3}$ x $28^{3}/_{4}$ inches (60 x 73cm)

(See caption on page 67)

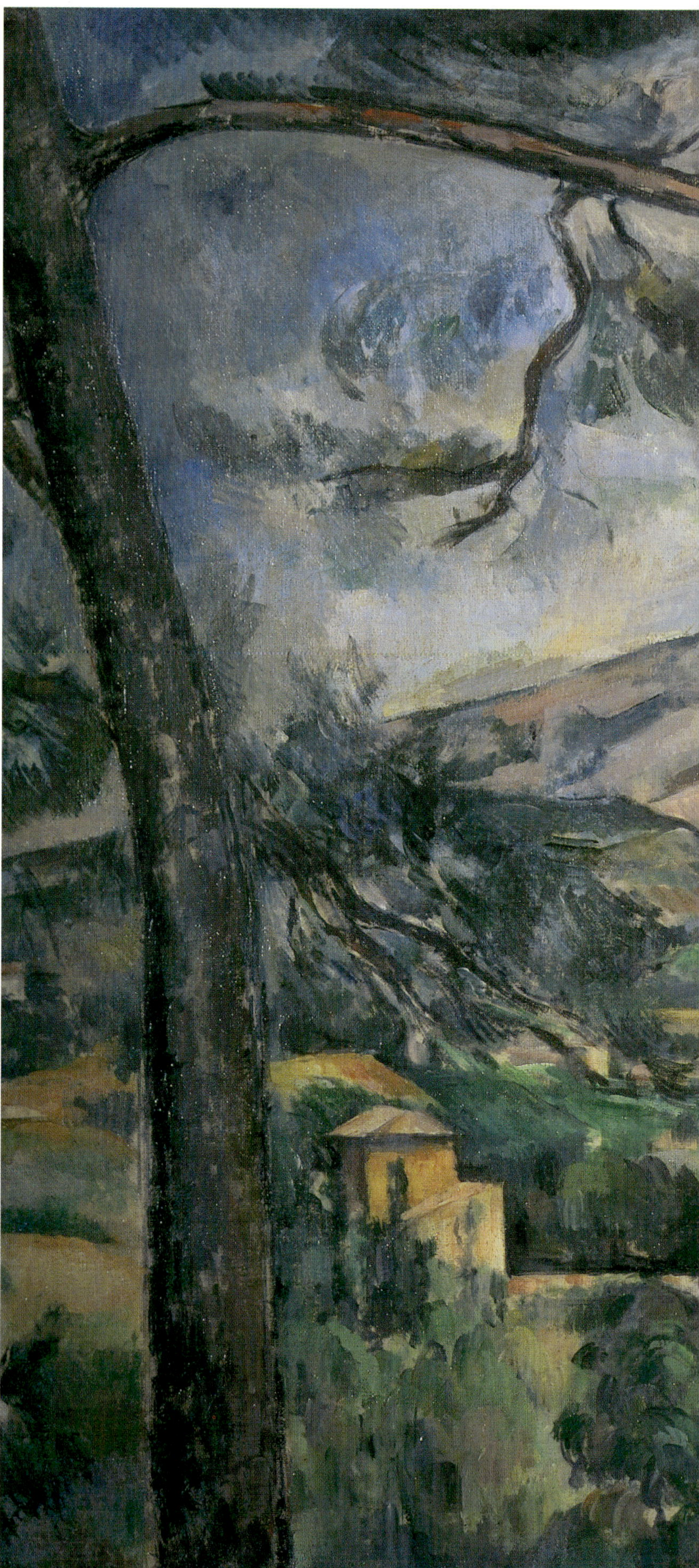

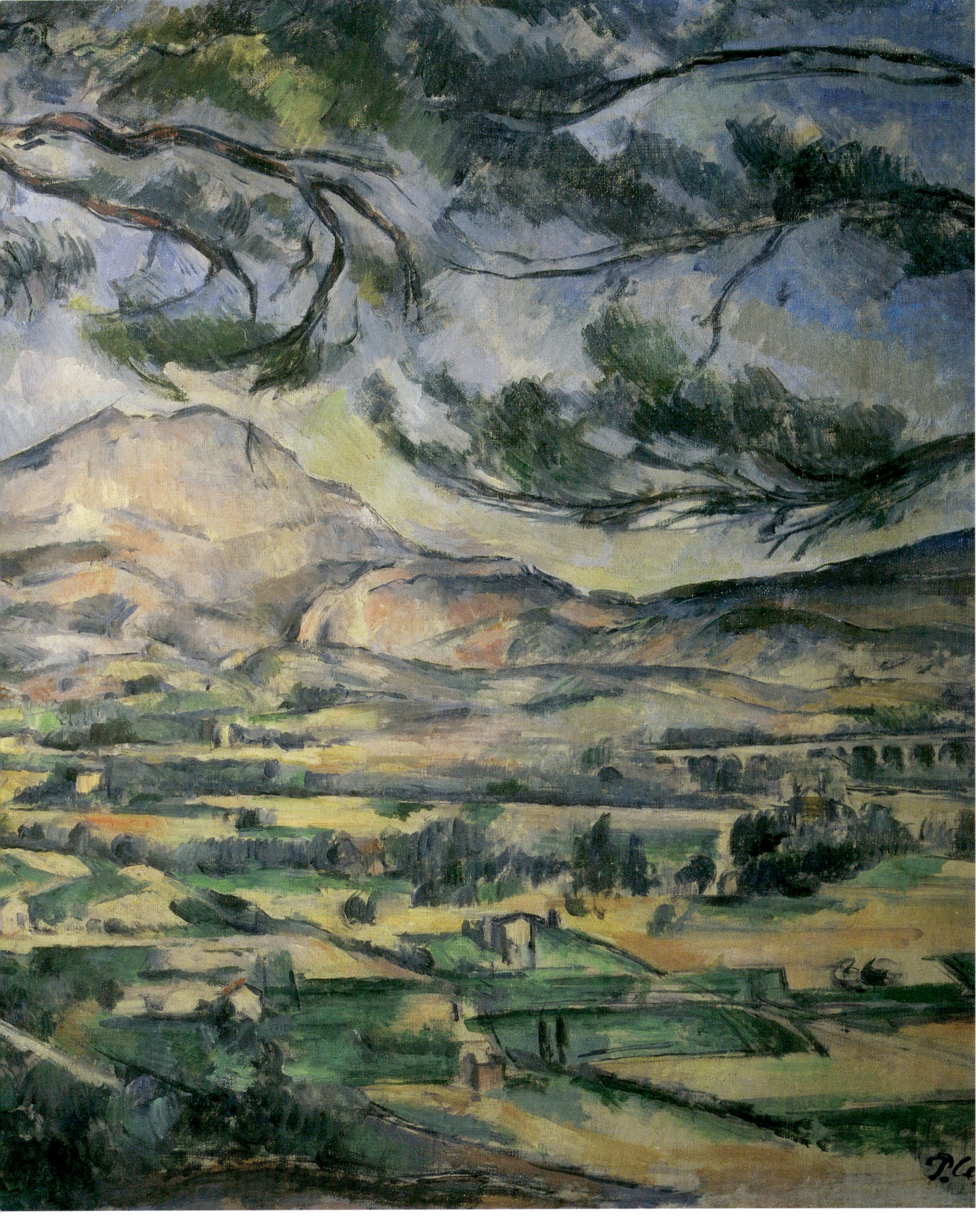

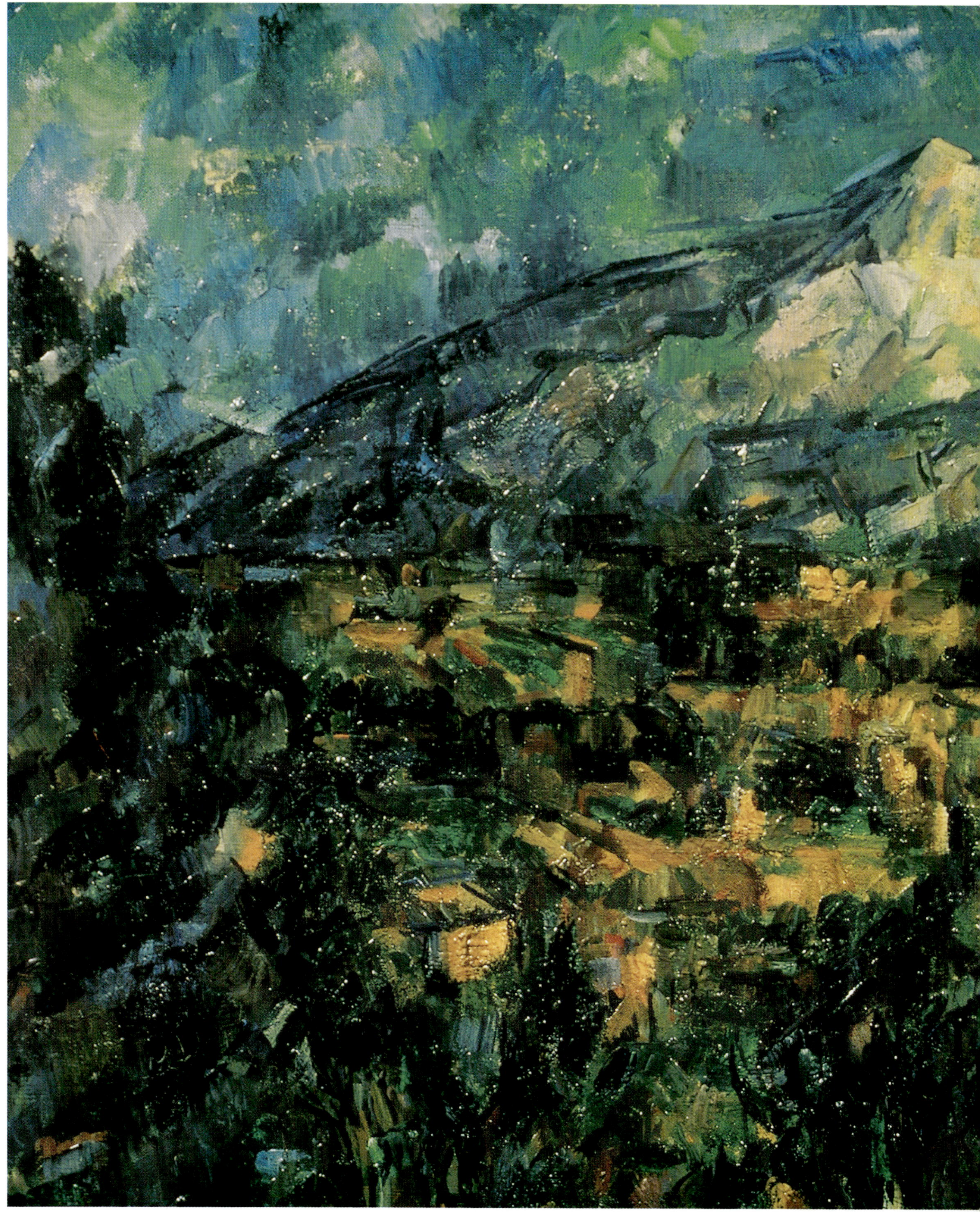

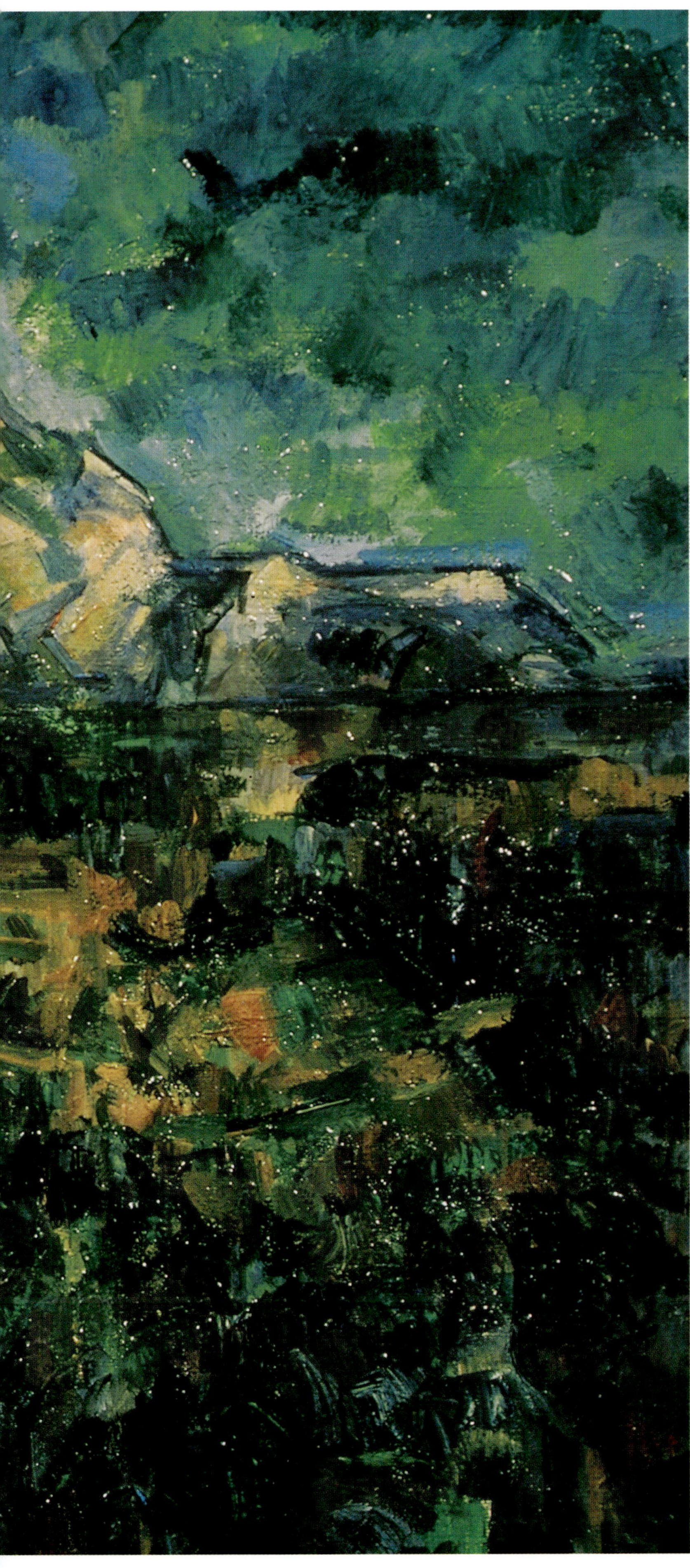

PLATE 44
Mont Sainte-Victoire (1904–06)
Oil on canvas, 25 x $32^{2}/_{3}$ inches (63.5 x 83cm)
(See caption on page 67)

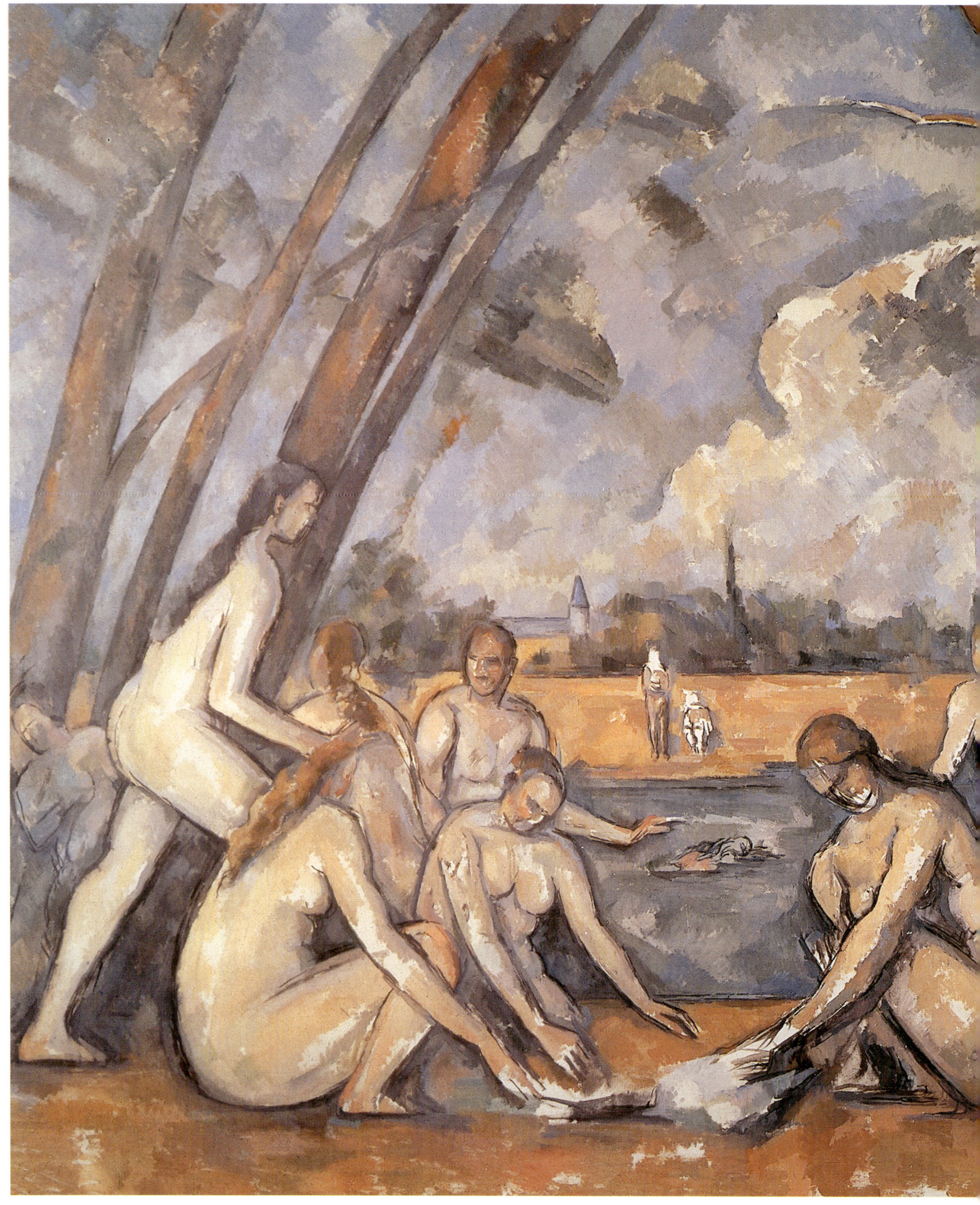

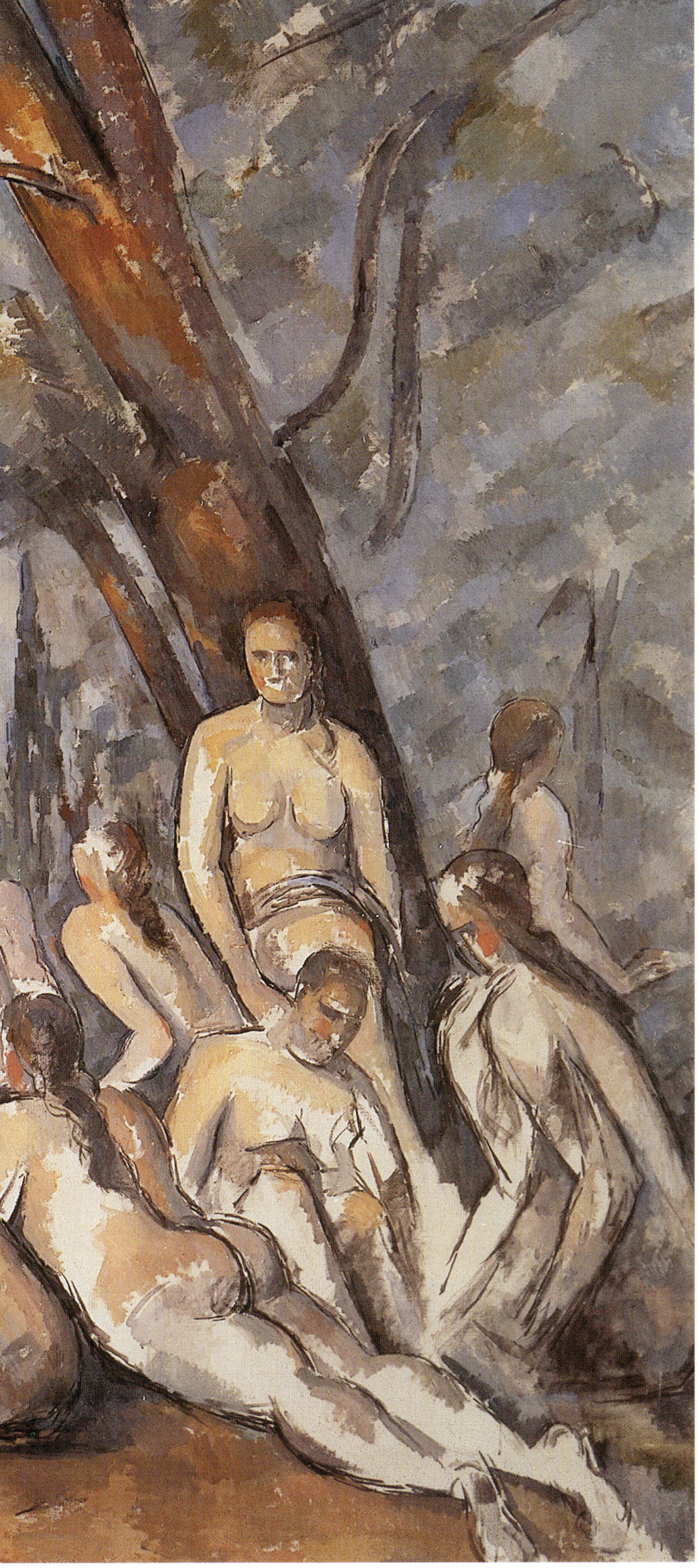

PLATE 45

Bathers (1902–06)

Oil on canvas, $81^{7}/_{8}$ x 98 inches (208 x 249cm)

During the last decade of his life, Cézanne returned to a subject that he had begun to explore in the 1880s – the construction of nude figure compositions that would extend the tradition of such historical paintings into his own pictorial aesthetic. In his earlier work he had used male figures and wished to construct the new studies with female nudes. This presented him with real problems, not the least because he was nervous of women and found it difficult to contemplate approaching them to ask them to remove their clothes; at best he thought he might get 'some very old flesh' (très vieille carne, *as he put it to Vollard, whose portrait he was painting when contemplating the nudes) to undertake this indelicate activity. In the event, he did make some studies from an older model but the main source for the figures he used were the drawings he had made at the Atelier Suisse many years earlier as a student and from his memory of the female body. It might be mentioned here that although his earlier drawings are academic in intention and keenly analytical and of great interest, they are not fluently constructed. Nevertheless, the figures represented in the paintings are not the result of an incapability of representing the human form in a traditional way but essentially because he was pursuing the same pictorial solutions, at the end of his life, that had concerned him since the last of his Impressionist paintings. These great works are a further presage of the 20th-century revolution represented by Cubism and Picasso's* Demoiselles d'Avignon, *in which the images present an analysis of the subject in the form of integrated elements derived from the necessary organization of the canvas surface to make a single unit. The awkwardness that appears in the figures comes from the unification of figures and landscape into a single object – an affecting painted area.*

It will not be necessary or possible to analyse these larger works of Cézanne's late career in a few words. Or indeed any number of words for any work of art. When all that can be said has been said, every work of art can still only ultimately speak in its own language; in this case, in paint and only the examination in visual terms that is not translatable will provide the real pictorial nourishment. These last paintings are difficult but finally enormously rewarding. It has already been noted that Cézanne found it difficult finally to finish a work and none of these Bathers is completed although he worked on them for over a decade. They demand and deserve the viewer's close attention. It will be well worth-while.

PLATE 46

Bathers (1906)

Oil on canvas, $51^{1}/_{4}$ x $76^{3}/_{4}$ inches (130 x 195cm)

(See caption on page 73)

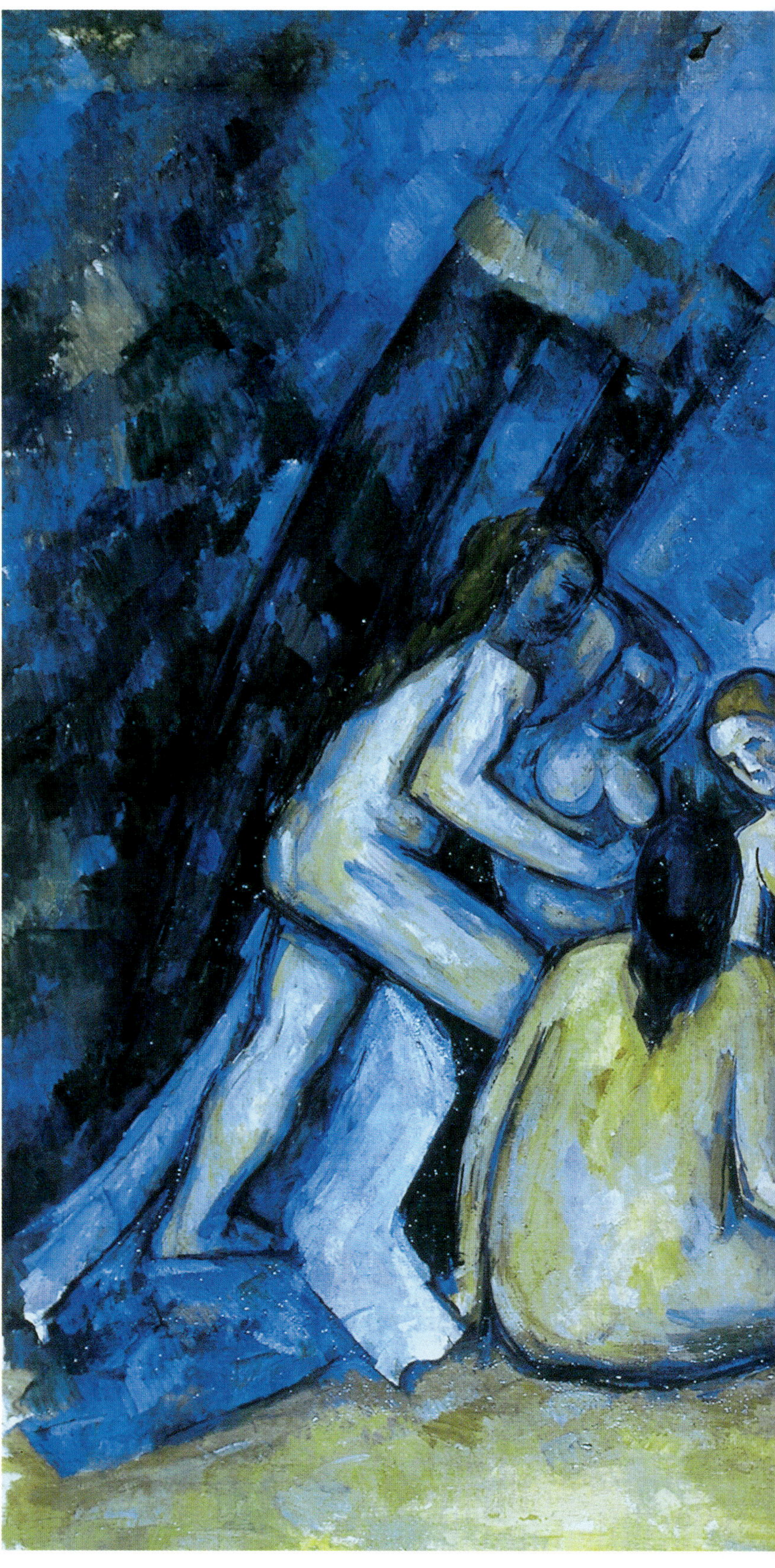

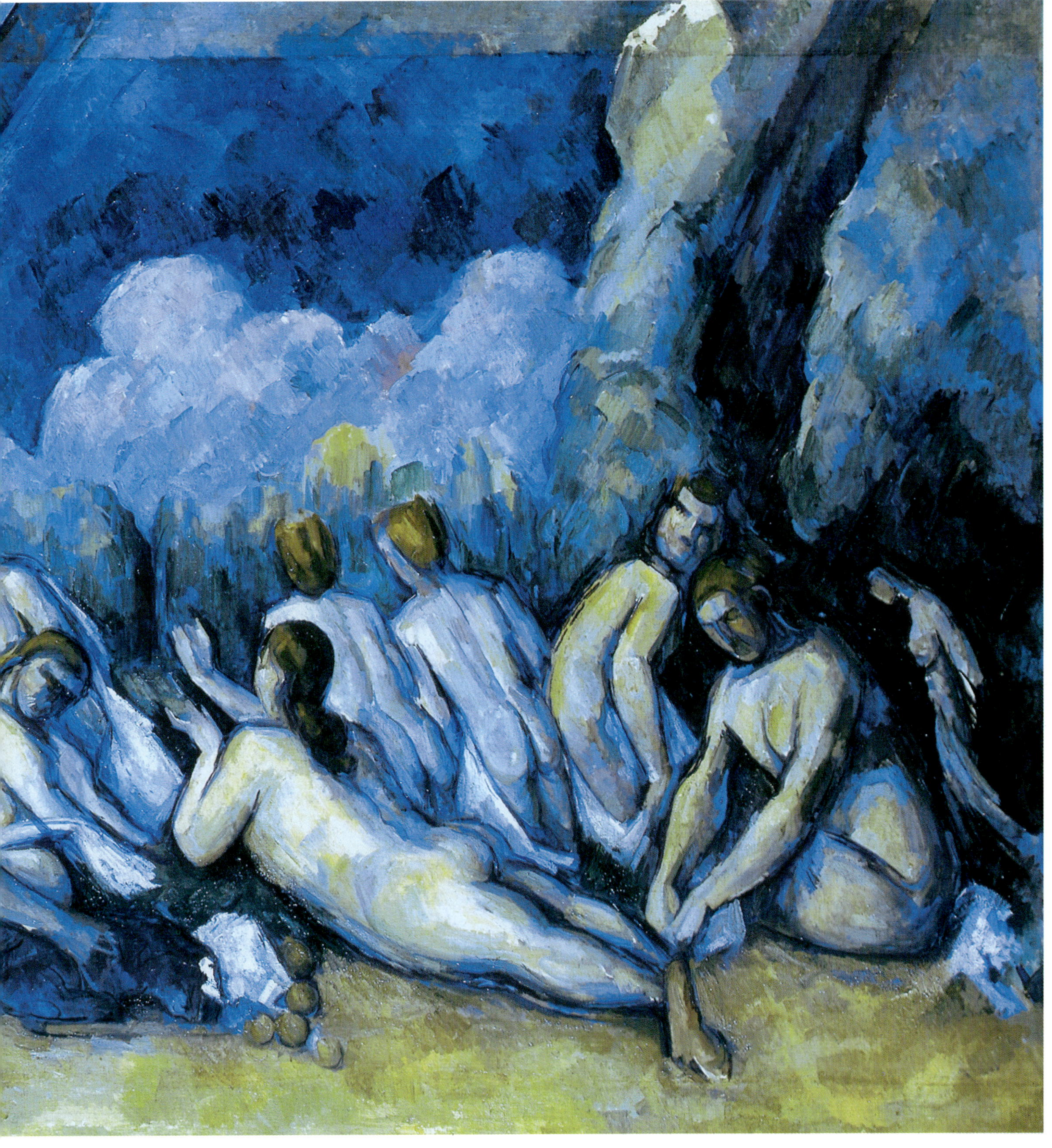

The Publishers wish to thank the following for providing photographs, and for permission to reproduce copyright material. While every effort has been made to trace and acknowledge copyright-holders, we wish to apologize should any omissions have been made.

Paul Cézanne
Hulton Images
Still-Life with Leg of Mutton and Bread
Kunsthaus, Zurich/Giraudon, Paris
Achille Emperaire
Musée d'Orsay/Giraudon, Paris
Head of an Old Man
Musée d'Orsay/Giraudon, Paris
A Modern Olympia
Musée d'Orsay/Giraudon, Paris
Still-Life with Green Pot and Pewter Jug
Musée d'Orsay/Lauros/Giraudon, Paris
The House of the Hanged Man, Auvers
Musée d'Orsay/Giraudon, Paris
Dr. Gachet's House in Auvers
Private Collection/Giraudon, Paris
Flowers in a Delft Vase
Private Collection
Dahlias
Musée d'Orsay/Lauros/Giraudon, Paris
Self-Portrait
Pushkin Museum, Moscow/Giraudon, Paris
Three Bathers
Musée du Petit-Palais, Paris/Giraudon, Paris
Self-Portrait
Musée d'Orsay/Lauros/Giraudon, Paris
Female Nude on Sofa
Von der Heydt Museum, Wuppertal/Giraudon, Paris
The Château at Médan
Art Gallery and Museum, Glasgow/Giraudon, Paris
Still-Life with Apples and Biscuits
Musée de l'Orangerie/Lauros/Giraudon, Paris
Still-Life with Apples and Biscuits
Private Collection/Giraudon, Paris
Poplars
Musée d'Orsay/Lauros/Giraudon, Paris
The Aqueduct
Pushkin Museum, Moscow/Giraudon, Paris
Still-Life with Fruits, Napkin and Milk Jug
Musée de l'Orangerie/Lauros/Giraudon, Paris
Mont Sainte-Victoire with Large Pine
Phillips' Collection, Washington D.C./Lauros/Giraudon, Paris
The Bay of Marseille seen from L'Estaque
Musée d'Orsay/Lauros/Giraudon, Paris
Pierrot and Harlequin
Pushkin Museum, Moscow/Giraudon, Paris
The Card Players
Courtauld Institute Galleries/Bridgeman, Giraudon, Paris
Man Smoking a Pipe
Courtauld Institute Galleries/Bridgeman, Giraudon, Paris
The Smoker
Stadtische Kunsthalle, Mannheim/Giraudon, Paris
The interior and exterior of Cézanne's studio in Aix-en-Provence (photograph)
Giraudon, Paris
An elderly Cézanne in his studio working on the *Large Bathers* (photograph)
Musée Marmottan/Giraudon, Paris
Still-Life of Pot of Flowers and Pears
Courtauld Institute Galleries/Bridgeman, Giraudon, Paris
The House of Bellevue
Private Collection/Giraudon, Paris
The Great Pine
Museum of Art, Sao Paulo/Giraudon, Paris
The Lac d'Annecy
Courtauld Institute Galleries/Bridgeman, Giraudon, Paris
Still-Life with Fruit Basket (The Kitchen Table)
Musée Marmottan/Giraudon, Paris
Peasant in a Blue Smock
Christie's, London/Bridgeman/Giraudon, Paris
Portrait of Madame Cézanne
Musée de l'Orangerie/Lauros/Giraudon, Paris
Woman in Blue
The Hermitage Museum, St. Petersburg/Giraudon, Paris
Self-Portrait in Felt Hat
Bridgestone Museum of Art, Tokyo/Giraudon, Paris
In the Grounds of the Château Noir
Musée de l'Orangerie/Lauros/Giraudon, Paris
The Bibémus Quarry
Sam Spiegel Collection, New York/Lauros/Giraudon, Paris
Still-Life with Apples and Oranges
Musée d'Orsay/Lauros/Giraudon, Paris
Portrait of Ambroise Vollard
Musée du Petit-Palais, Paris/Giraudon, Paris
Mont Sainte-Victoire
Kunsthaus, Zurich/Giraudon, Paris
Mont Sainte-Victoire from Les Lauves
Courtauld Institute Galleries/Bridgeman, Giraudon, Paris
Mont Sainte-Victoire
Pushkin Museum, Moscow/Giraudon, Paris
Bathers
Philadelphia Museum of Art/Bridgeman, Giraudon, Paris
Bathers
The National Gallery, London/Bridgeman, Giraudon, Paris